Buy to Let in Spain

Thank you for buying one of our books. We hope you'll enjoy the book, and that it will help you to realise the ideal combination of a place in the sun and a rising investment.

We always try to ensure our books are up to date, but contact details seem to change so quickly that it can be very hard to keep up with them. If you do have any problems contacting any of the organisations listed at the back of the book please get in touch, and either we or the author will do what we can to help. And if you do find correct contact details that differ from those in the book, please let us know so that we can put it right when we reprint.

Please do also give us your feedback so we can go on making books that you want to read. If there's anything you particularly liked about this book – or you have suggestions about how it could be improved in the future – email us on info@howtobooks.co.uk

For further information on the property market both in Spain and the UK you can subscribe to www.propertyhotspots.net for up to the minute information on property hotspots, property prices, rental yields, property search, estate agents, letting agents, auctions, 100% mortgage providers, buy-to-let mortgage providers, portfolio management, and much more.

The Publishers
www.howtobooks.co.uk

If you want to know how. . .

Buying a Property in Spain
An insider guide to realising your dream

Going to Live in Spain
A practical guide to enjoying a new lifestyle in the sun

Buy to Let in France
How to invest in French property for pleasure and profit

Starting & Running a B&B in France
*How to make money and have fun running your
own chambres d'hote*

Retire Abroad
Your complete guide to a new life in the sun

howtobooks

Please send for a free copy of the latest catalogue:

How To Books
3 Newtec Place, Magdalen Road
Oxford OX4 1RE, United Kingdom
email: info@howtobooks.co.uk
http://www.howtobooks.co.uk

Buy to Let in Spain

*How to invest in Spanish property
for pleasure and profit*

HARRY KING

howtobooks

First published in 2003 by
How To Books Ltd
3 Newtec Place, Magdalen Road
Oxford OX4 1RE, United Kingdom.
Tel: (01865) 793806. Fax: (01865) 248780.
email: info@howtobooks.co.uk
http://www.howtobooks.co.uk

British Library Cataloguing in Publication Data
A catalogue record for this book is available from the British
Library

Illustrations by Nickie Averill
Cover design by Baseline Arts Ltd, Oxford
Produced for How To Books by Deer Park Productions
Typeset by PDQ Typesetting, Newcastle-under-Lyme, Staffs.
Printed and bound by Cromwell Press, Trowbridge, Wiltshire

NOTE: The material contained in this book is set out in good
faith for general guidance and no liability can be accepted
for loss or expense incurred as a result of relying in particular
circumstances on statements made in the book. The laws and
regulations are complex and liable to change, and readers should
check the current position with the relevant authorities before
making personal arrangements.

Contents

List of Illustrations

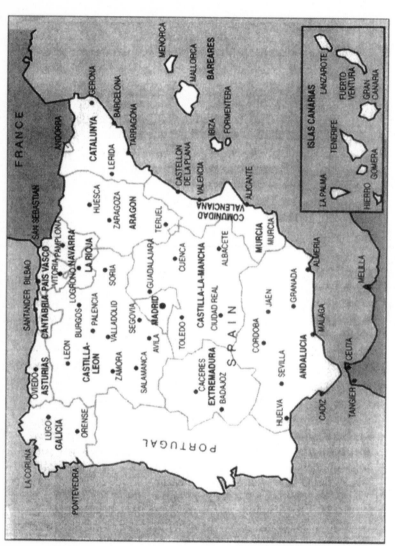

Figure 1. A map of Spain.

Preface

Today's Spain is a young vibrant country. No land is so diverse or enjoys such an excellent climate. It has a strong personality, is full of rich traditions and has a totally unique culture. Tourism has changed its face forever. Fishing villages have been replaced with skyscraper hotel blocks. Yet only a few kilometres inland towns and villages lie untouched, retaining their own distinctive lifestyle. The old links to agriculture still exist. Orange and lemon groves, almond trees, thousands of acres of vines and millions of olive trees still remain.

Spain has many sides to its character. Visit the incomparable Alhambra in Granada where Jews, Christians and Arabs once lived in peace. Birds of prey soar high over the castles of the Costa Blanca. In spring the pink and white almond trees blossom profusely. Orange, lemon and cherry trees add additional colour with the red wild poppies. Ancient windmills are silhouetted against the blue sky. In autumn the browns change to a purple green as the countryside softens with the advent of gentle rain.

Of course there are the Spaniards themselves. Cordial people. A loquacious race, they can be friendly, enthusiastic, and tolerant all at once. Charming people as they are, they tend to speak very rapidly in a regional language which seems to be quite different to the Spanish learned at night school back home. They have a different body clock too. They can be noisy, eating at some ungodly late hour. Then there are the frustrating delays. People do not rush about. If you need something repaired, it often takes longer than it should. But people adjust and learn to be patient. It is important to understand the Spanish mentality and their way of life. Don't dash about, learn to relax, live for today and not tomorrow.

Spain is also Europe's biggest holiday playground, playing host to some 50 million foreign visitors each year. They enjoy the delights of a traditional family holiday on the Islands or the Costas. Many explore the deep green pastures and cities of northern Spain, or sample the rural way of life. They may soak up the sun, look at the sights or partake in outdoor activities. Spain – so many things to do and so many places to see. There are the endless days of sunshine, incomparable scenery, beaches of fine sand, high mountains, vast plains, balmy moonlight evenings, good wine, many fine restaurants and a variety of nightlife.

Visitors to Spain stay in the many thousands of tourist hotels and now in the new breed of macro hotels each with upwards of 1,500 beds. The tourist industry is also justifiably proud of its unique hotels called *Paradores*, the majority of which are restored historic monuments such as castles, monasteries, convents or palaces, with great care taken to preserve their decor and distinctive characteristics. Accommodation can additionally be provided by hostels, pensions, spas, guesthouses, farmhouses, inns, campsites, timeshares, holiday homes and rented property.

People who own a holiday home in Spain may be interested in letting it out in order to provide an income to cover running costs and to help with mortgage payments. It is highly unlikely however that all outgoings will be met from rental income as the holiday season is too short and there is simply too much competition. The holiday letting season is longest in the Canaries where properties have year-round letting potential.

Enter the new breed of buy-to-let property owners. They are not commercial property developers since they wish to enjoy the benefits of their purchase too. But they do recognise the conundrum that a home is bought with the heart, a commercial property with the head and a Buy to Let property for Fun and Profit.

In almost any community in the world, the richest people are almost invariably the landlords, people who own property and rent it out to others. Landlording is probably the world's second oldest profession. How many times have you heard someone say, 'If only I had bought that property years ago I'd be wealthy today?' While most people believe property is the best way to keep up with and get ahead of inflation, too many potential buyers just talk about investing and do not take the first step of buying a second property.

Most homeowners have watched the value of their property skyrocket, and dream of their wealth. The problem with that, of course, is that they always need a place to live, so if their house is sold and a profit taken, they still need another and usually more expensive home to live in. As a result, some of these owners have realised that the way to succeed is to buy a second, third, or more homes. That way they can treat the other properties as true investments and cash in on the profits.

Property has not always increased in value. Following the Lawson boom-years property values increased rapidly, and fell just as abruptly in 1996. This was the first major property recession since the end of World War II. There will always be short-term booms and some recessions but the prospect for long-term steady growth seems excellent.

If it's so easy to make money by owning income property, why aren't more people landlords? Why is it that the average person shies away from getting involved? A lack of knowledge is probably the greatest deterrent. People need to know how to get started, how to buy right, and how to finance a purchase with little or no money down. Tenants are the second major reason why people are afraid to become property investors. They've heard all the horror stories about unpaid rent, late night complaints, vandalism, and all the other bad things that can come with letting property.

The key to successful long-term property investment is to let a property for its annual costs. If this can be done then the property essentially pays for itself, as each year it is owned its value goes up. But to do this the property must be in a good location, have a plentiful supply of good tenants and the owner must learn to be a good landlord.

Property in Spain is not expensive. It is quite different and the choice is great. Houses with distinctive styles are built on urbanisations, on individual plots or scattered on hillsides. Many enjoy distinctive country houses known as *fincas* and traditional town houses. Buyers want homes to enjoy for themselves and their families – for fun and income.

Spanish buying procedures are also very different. Forget the traditional approach of putting in an 'offer', arranging a mortgage and asking your solicitor to sort things out. Prospective buyers must carry out research and ask questions themselves, rather than assuming a solicitor will deal with these matters. Learn about the *Abogado,* the *Notary*, and the *Gestor*. It will make things so much easier. It is necessary to understand the Spanish conveyancing system from start to finish. It can trap the unwary in a country where there are many property horror stories.

This book is not for property speculators. The aim is to help buy-to-let investors seek their first property in Spain, impart knowledge and deal with some anticipated problems.

Harry King
Pedreguer, Spain

Acknowledgements

I am grateful for the information supplied by Dr Tony Warnes at Sheffield University, Russell King at the University of Sussex and Allan Williams at the University of Exeter. Their study of why people move from the United Kingdom to Mediterranean locations is encapsulated in their book *Sunset Lives*. It is the only source of quantified facts on this issue.

Valencia Communidad, the Spanish Tourist Board, Halifax PLC, the *Financial Times* and Gibraltar Airways responded to requests for information. Chloride, a small mining town in Nevada USA, unexpectedly provided an American view of letting on a large scale.

Once again I would like to thank my partner Joan Stock for her support and contribution, translating documents from Spanish to English and checking the final manuscript for facts, omissions and errors. Her son Chris owns the property in Castell de Castells featured as the main case study throughout the book.

Lastly I would like to thank the numerous people who provided information and those who allowed their own experiences to be published as case studies. To protect the innocent some names and places have been changed.

$$\left(\,1\,\right)$$

Buying Property is a Good Idea

Why do we always get mixed messages from the business pages of quality newspapers? House prices are going up. High street spending is good. Retail prices are declining. Unemployment is down. High salaries are being earned. Individually we are all in good shape. Or are we? Shares are down! Pensions depressed! Annuities are lower!

However it is better than the early 1990s when short-term interest rates were 15%, ten year Government bonds paid more than 9% p.a. and dividends from the largest UK blue chip companies were 5%. In September 1992 the Pound was forced out of the dreaded Exchange Rate Mechanism that supported the high interest policy of the German Bundesbank.

The greatest Bull Run in history ended in March 2000. Shares soared by more than 1,000% between 1982 and the peak in December 1999. A couple of months later, the tech bubble burst and equities began their long slide.

Today the major stock markets remain volatile and are predicted to remain so. It is widely accepted that America leads the world's economic growth. The FTSE seems to follow the NASDAC like a shadow and September the 11th hangs like a cloud over us all. Volatility makes share price predictions impossible.

The same applies to house prices. One day it is announced that house prices will go through the roof. The next day they are about to crash. Can you believe anything the property experts claim? Try to gain enlightenment from *Private Eye*'s headline 'House Prices Slump to Their Highest Level Ever'.

The truth is that nobody knows whether house prices will go up or down.

There is a bullish case. When interest rates are at their low level and when not enough new homes are being built to meet demand, money will continue to flow into bricks and mortar as people come to realise what a poor return they have received on their shares and building society accounts.

There is a bearish case. Property is echoing the dotcom bubble – the market is being driven up by fad and fashion, and bust will inevitably follow. Speculation it may be but it is notoriously hard to predict.

SHOULD YOU BUY PROPERTY OR SHARES?

Deciding whether to invest in property or shares has never been more difficult. Since 1982, shares have been the star performers. The average property has increased in value by 319% while shares have risen more than 600%. Over ten years share prices went up by 142% compared with a 96% growth in property prices. Only from 2000, when the tech bubble burst, did property beat equities.

However, over the long term the picture is more even. In the past 50 years, house prices and the stock market have risen by almost exactly the same amount on an averaged annual basis. Houses have increased by an average of 8.2% per year and the capital value of shares by 8.3% per year. If dividends are taken into account, however, shares have an advantage.

History suggests that markets and assets move in cycles, in which case house prices and share prices will at some point converge again. The question is whether they meet because house prices fall or because shares go up.

This demonstrates a need for a balanced portfolio.

Property

More people are buying their own homes than at any time since the late 1980s. They are concerned that if they do not get on the property ladder soon, property will become too expensive. The outlook for the market appears fairly sound. The population is growing but fewer homes are being built than at any time since the 1930s. When demand outstrips supply, prices usually rise. The increase in the number of single owner-occupiers has further boosted demand. Interest rates are low, so homes are more affordable.

Shares
One of the key measures of a share's value is its price-earnings (p/e) ratio, which compares share prices with earnings, or profits, per share. The British market has a p/e ratio average over the past 20 years of 13, so share prices are 13 times the average company's earnings per share. In America the 20-year average p/e ratio is 16 and in Europe it is 14.

Any deviation up or down from this average suggests that the market is either over or undervalued. With a growth of 6% a year and a p/e ratio of 13 it will still take until 2006 for the FTSE100 to reach its 2001 peak.

PROPERTY INVESTMENT IS BETTER THAN A PENSION
Thousands of people saving for retirement have turned to property because of high property inflation and crisis in the pensions industry. Personal pensions were mis-sold by commission-hungry salesmen in the 1980s, leaving the industry a massive compensation bill. The downfall of Equitable Life, which managed the pensions of thousands of people, also tarnished the industry's reputation.

Pension values have slumped as the stock market has fallen. At the same time, house prices have soared, prompting many savers to look to property as an alternative.

Pensions can be highly inflexible. Most of the fund is used to buy an annuity, which provides an income for life, by the age of 75. It is not normal to withdraw money from a pension fund until at least 50 years of age. Annuity rates are lower for people who retire early. Another drawback with a pension is that annuity providers keep the money, so on death, it cannot be bequeathed to heirs.

Buying a property to let has become a popular alternative to pensions because returns are so strong, but caution is necessary because rents can fall and investors can find it harder to pay their mortgages. Buy to Let investors are also urged to be realistic about capital growth.

UNDERSTANDING LEVERAGE

Leverage means investing the least possible amount of personal capital when buying a property in order to earn the maximum percentage return on the invested amount. In other words, leveraging means borrowing money.

In property, thanks to leverage, the owner controls the entire property even though personal equity invested may be only 10% to 25% of the purchase price. The ultimate leverage of all is of course no cash down payment at all, with a 100% mortgage.

No alternative business proposition allows such a small down payment percentage without corresponding disadvantages. Property leverage lets the investor get the entire benefit from the property's appreciation in market value with only small cash investment. Should the investment lose value, which rarely happens in sound, well-located property, the investor's risk is limited to the down payment.

Leverage is the insider's secret that maximises the smart investor's return on investment. A property worth 300,000 Euros with an 85% mortgage on the value of a home needs a deposit of 45,000 Euros and mortgage interest repayments of 1,275 Euros per month at 6%. A rent of 1,800 Euros per month is required to cover tax and other costs. This is an income of 7.2% of the property value, which is quite respectable in any situation and maintains a positive cash flow. With property inflation at say 10%, a healthy profit is achieved. And the bonus ... the property remains the owner's. It can be passed to heirs as a flexible investment.

MORTGAGES ARE GETTING CHEAPER

The Bank of England base rate fell to 4% in 2002, which means borrowers have enjoyed the lowest interest rates in almost 40 years (see Figure 2). A typical standard variable rate would be around 6%. Mortgages keep getting cheaper as lenders fight for discounted business. Compare this to the 15% of ten years ago.

There are often better deals in the marketplace. It may pay to transfer a mortgage and this is particularly worthwhile if increasing the size of a mortgage to release some equity from an existing property in order to buy a second one abroad.

Year	Average UK Inflation Rate	Average UK Mortgage Rate
1996	2.45%	7.35%
1997	3.10%	7.90%
1998	3.40%	8.65%
1999	1.55%	7.20%
2000	2.95%	7.60%
1001	1.85%	6.70%
2002	1.20%	5.75%

Figure 2. UK inflation and mortgage rates.

Lenders in Britain are quite relaxed about homeowners using the equity in their UK homes to fund the purchase of a second property overseas. Most people who are looking to buy overseas have a lot of equity. As long as the repayments are affordable, extending the UK mortgage should not be a problem.

In addition to Spanish banks, a number of British banks, through their Spanish or Gibraltar based subsidiaries, now offer mortgages on properties in Spain. Financing a property in Spain does offer more options than a straightforward mortgage extension on a UK home. Less risk is achieved by borrowing in Euros. When currencies move, the asset will move in the same direction as the mortgage.

KEEPING LIQUID

When making any investment consider liquidity. It is defined as the time delay required to convert an asset into cash. For example, common stocks listed on the Stock

Exchange are considered relatively liquid since they can be sold and converted into cash within three or four days at most. But the cost of that liquidity is that the stock is sold at its market price on the day of the sale, and the investor has no control over what that price will be.

Many people think the biggest drawback of property investment is its lack of liquidity. It is certainly not as liquid as a savings account. But good property can be sold within 30 to 90 days for its true market value. However, due to unrealistic pricing by many sellers property sales often take a long time.

But there is another aspect to property liquidity. It is refinancing. Except in times of extremely tight mortgage money, which is experienced cyclically, most good property can be refinanced to produce liquid cash. A major advantage of refinancing a mortgage, instead of selling a property, is that refinancing is free from capital gains tax. Mortgage refinancing giving liquidity is an advantage most other investments lack.

So property is really more liquid than most people think.

PROPERTY IS THE BEST INVESTMENT IN THE WORLD

Andrew Carnegie said, 'Ninety per cent of all millionaires become so by owning property.' More money has been made in property than in all industrial investments combined. Why? Property values do not depend upon emotions but upon the hard facts of supply and demand.

A buy-to-let property, when properly purchased and correctly managed, but then sold if it gives an unsatisfactory financial return, offers the greatest economic benefit of any form of investment.

Buying your first home or umpteenth investment property should always be viewed as an investment. If the property gives pride of ownership and a lot of fun, that is great. But never buy just for emotional benefits. Emotional decisions have no place in property purchases. If a home is not purchased as an investment first, and as a place to live second, it can easily turn into a losing proposition.

Unlike the stock or commodities markets, the property market value is to some extent under the owner's control. If a person thinks a particular property is worth a certain amount then that is the money paid. But buyers and sellers of common stocks and commodities are at the mercy of other traders in the marketplace.

And of course there is inflation. Even in a recession, house prices in most communities will continue rising. There will be a few local exceptions, such as areas where a major employer closes a factory, but except for these situations the price of new and resale homes will keep going up.

BUYING ABROAD

With house prices increasing rapidly homeowners are now sitting on a valuable asset. Many have released some of the equity they have built up during the housing boom to acquire rental properties abroad. The reasons are simple. They are worried the housing market in the UK is beginning to look precarious. They believe that a smarter move is to use the spare cash to buy a holiday home in Spain, France or Italy.

The weather in Europe is obviously a big attraction, but lower property prices have helped to fuel the boom. French property is typically a third cheaper, and Spanish property is half the price of an equivalent home in Britain.

Buying overseas also makes more sense these days because of the increased availability and convenience of cheap flights.

SPANISH PROPERTY PRICE INCREASES

Despite a massive building programme, Spain's property prices over the last 20 years have risen higher than any other industrialised nation in the world. Since 1980 the cost of buying a property has risen by a staggering 726%. In the last four years house prices have risen by 66%, increasing in the last 12 months by 14% for new homes and 18% for used homes.

The surge began with the need to spend cash piles before the introduction of the Euro and prices have continued to rise because of the sharp decline in stocks and shares. Property has also become the major focus of investment for companies through trusts and individuals looking to earn profits from their savings.

As a consequence however, Spanish families are in debt to a level never previously experienced due to the disparity between property prices and wage levels, which have risen only marginally in the last four years and remain low in comparison to the rest of Europe.

Figure 3 compares Spanish and UK property inflation to that of UK equities over a common 20 year period.

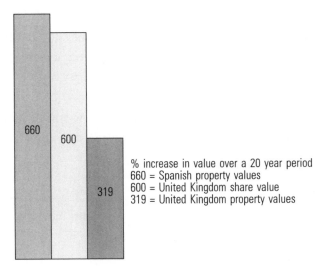

660

600

319

% increase in value over a 20 year period
660 = Spanish property values
600 = United Kingdom share value
319 = United Kingdom property values

Figure 3. Property versus shares.

CASE STUDY – CASTLES IN THE AIR

If any one was upwardly mobile it was Chris, 30 years of age, single, good-looking and a well paid account executive of an international computer company. That is not to say the salary was not well deserved, for it was a demanding occupation necessitating planned periods of relaxation through rugby, running, music, the inevitable partying and regular trips to Spain to see his parents who were resident a few miles inland from the Costa Blanca. Chris knew Spain too. He had taken two years out working in and around the coastal town of Javea.

He decided to invest in an additional property. Why not! His shares were declining. Property prices were increasing rapidly worldwide. Buy-to-let was a rising market and the newspapers were full of its advantages. And the all-important figures! In the UK about 5% of loans advanced were now for buy-to-let investors – 100,000 people in total per year. Perhaps the UK market would decline? On investigation it was possible to borrow money on the value of his home from his existing UK building society who knew it would go towards an overseas property.

Although Chris knew by now a buy-to-let would be better if it were in Spain rather than Scarbourgh or Saltcoats the question was – where in Spain? He looked at the prestigious Olive Nova Golf Course designed by Seve Ballesteros but it was deserted in winter. Javea, a pretty town, was being spoiled by overdevelopment. Nothing was gelling. Where was this elusive property?

Chris's mother found it! A partly modernised, but unfinished house in the mountain village of Castell de Castells an hours drive from the Costas. It was a big job, planning the work, writing the building specification, getting the builders in and dealing with the wearisome buying procedures. Purchasing furniture, ordering a new kitchen, hanging the lights and buying the fittings all came later. However, willing parents oversaw all these tasks with a Power of Attorney drawn up at the Spanish Consulate in London paving the way.

Chris now relaxes surrounded by an amphitheatre of mountains, which reach to over 1,750 metres and have ruined castles on their tops. The village has narrow, steep streets barely passable by motorcar. It is a well-known beauty spot, a centre for walking on forestry paths, mule tracks and ancient trails.

The property is let to hikers from England or America – such is the power of the internet – organised by his parents of course.

(Readers can follow this case study in Chapter 5 – A Special Place and in the Business Plan in Appendix 6.)

LIVING IN A GLOBAL ECONOMY

Today we live in a global economy. The British, Spanish and European economies follow the American economy step for step, subject to any variation caused by a localised opportunity or threat. Europe is bound together not only geographically, but also politically, economically and socially to the prosperity of the dollar.

In the USA the decline of mortgage interest rates has also propped up the market for homes. With mortgage rates low, it is hard to have a low demand housing market in America. When interest rates start to climb upward the market will cool, but a relatively tight supply of homes for sale and population trends will ensure a steady stream of likely buyers will end up paying top dollar.

The buy-to-let property market can be in Pounds, Euros or Dollars. The property can be in the UK, Spain or the United States. The principals, opportunities and risks are all similar.

SUMMARY

- It is difficult to predict the growth rates of shares and property.

- Shares still seem to have an edge over property, but like everything else it depends on the starting point.

- Pensions are not a good investment with annuity rates so low. For the adventurous property is a better bet.

- A mortgaged property offers better leverage and greater liquidity than any other business venture.

- Compared with ten years ago, mortgages are cheap. In the natural cycle of events they may rise from their current levels, but not to the rates of a decade ago.

- Buying abroad has natural attractions and with Spanish property inflation being the highest in the world, financial attractions too.

- Whatever happens in Spain and the UK, it is as followers of the dollar.

Understanding Letting

DO YOU REALLY WANT TO BE A LANDLORD?

Starting up and running a business demands skill, knowledge, commitment, drive and self-motivation. While it is possible to run a Spanish let from the UK many successful lets are run by local people who are prepared to put in that extra personal effort in caring for their tenants. Being a landlord does not mean under-taking the day-to-day work personally as someone else can be employed to do it. What attributes are necessary for a successful landlord?

It does help to know something about property – the structure, the design of brickwork and the general things that builders get up to. But first and foremost the idea of owning property must appeal. If you love cars buy cars. If you love mountains live there. To own property you must be passionate about it.

It helps to be businesslike and efficient, prepared to accept an element of risk, with good people management skills, a problem-solving turn of mind and the ability to respond to new situations. Better to be an extrovert, rather than introvert.

The most important business skill is to be comfortable with the numbers when understanding profitability and risks. Be aware of legal and tax obligations. Practical skills come into it too! The more skills available the greater likelihood of keeping costs down.

THE STIGMA OF RACHMANISM

Few landlords can compare with Peter Rachman. During the 1950s, Rachman, an expatriate Pole, bought hundreds of slum properties in the now-fashionable West London areas of Notting Hill and Bayswater, and let them out mainly to newly arrived Jamaican immigrants who found it difficult to get accommodation of any kind. Rachman overcrowded and overcharged his many tenants, and then enforced his rule by means of hired thugs. His tenants had no recourse to the law and were in any case grateful for having a roof over their heads. Rachman, who began life as a landlord by finding rooms for prostitutes, became a multi-millionaire by this means. He has been immortalised, however, by an entry in the Oxford English Dictionary, where 'Rachmanism' is defined as 'exploitation of slum tenants by unscrupulous landlords'.

To this day, anybody who buys a property to let, thus becoming a landlord, risks being called a Rachman with its word-association of evil. The term stigmatises landlords for ever as being greedy, exploitative and amoral. Even the nicest landladies can sometimes hear themselves being called Rachman.

There may still be some mini-Rachmans in existence, as no amount of legislation can thwart those who are really determined. Today's typical landlords are most likely to have one or two rental properties, furnished with as much care and taste as their own home who are looking to make a safe, steady extra income. Present-day landlords often view their rental properties as a sideline while continuing with a day job.

INTO THE 90S

In the United Kingdom
The letting market has moved on from the 50s through successive legislation designed to equalise supply and demand in the marketplace, giving fairness to both the tenant and landlord for security of tenure and price inflation increases.

1957 saw the first of a number of UK Rent Acts where tenants could no longer be turned out on a whim, but were protected by law. If they felt they were paying too high a rent, or that their landlord was not keeping the place in good repair, tenants could apply to a Rent Tribunal for a fair rent that, in effect, meant a vastly decreased rent. The fair rent decided on by the tribunal was usually considerably less than the market rent for that particular property. Rent Acts shifted the balance of power so much in the tenant's favour that before long nobody wanted to be a private landlord. By the 1980s what remained of the private rented sector was highly undesirable as properties available for rent were usually dilapidated, dingy and in poor repair.

The 1988 UK Housing Act introduced changes intended to make the rented sector fairer for both landlords and tenants, and bring more rental properties onto the market. It gave potential landlords the confidence to start letting again by introducing the concept of the Assured Shorthold Tenancy, a legally binding agreement whereby properties were let out for six months at a time and capable of termination by either party so long as due notice each way had been given and accepted. Rents could only be increased on a yearly basis.

In Spain
Spain too has had its problems with letting laws following a similar but later version of the UK pattern. Under the rental laws from 1964 to 1985 tenants were so protected that landlords more or less gave up, which led to a critical housing shortage. These old laws protected tenants so strongly they could pass on their rights to children and grandchildren. Furthermore, the rent could never be raised, or only by a fraction of the inflation rate. Tenants refused to vacate and were entitled to an extension of their contract, regardless of the landlord's desire to end the letting and recover his property. Landlords left their apartments empty rather than risk the dangers of a sitting tenant and refused to repair the crumbling buildings that brought them no profit.

Of course things had to change and revised rental laws passed in 1985 aimed to remedy this situation by making rental properties good business. The revised law provided that all contracts ended when they said they would end, without provision for forcible extension. The law also ended any restrictions on rent increases. So the pendulum swung. Rents began to rise and short-term contracts with little protection for the tenant were offered. Now it was the tenants who suffered.

Enter the last piece of legislation, the 1995 law called the *Ley de Arrendamientos*, designed to provide a better balance between the rights and needs of tenants and landlords and to at last bring a final solution to the generations of sitting tenants under the 1964/85 laws that all but ruined the Spanish rental property market. The new law ends the forcible extension of rental contracts indefinitely renewable by the tenant and allows a landlord to raise the old low rents and to recover their own property. It provides tenants with more security than the 1985 law, obliging landlords to renew residential rental contracts for up to five years. It also establishes the landlord's right to a deposit of one month's rent for an unfurnished property and two months rent for a furnished property as a guarantee against damages. A third party can hold the deposit independent of both landlord and tenant.

The contract for a long-term rental is called *Arrienda de Vivienda*. The law provides for long-term rentals to be of up to five years duration. If the landlord offers a contract of three years duration, which is accepted, and then the tenant wishes to stay on for another two years it is automatically renewed on the same terms. If the tenant wishes to leave after three years then the contract is terminated. Annual rent increases in line with inflation take place during the contracted term. A new level of rent is set at the commencement of a new contract.

Short-term rental contracts are called *Arrienda de Temporada.* The straightforward, standard contract is in Spanish or in English, or both languages, for a specific period of time at a stated price. The renewal of the contract is at the landlord's discretion.

More details of Spanish contracts are contained in Chapter 10.

BUY-TO-LET IN THE UK

A major factor that has revolutionised rental properties in the UK has been the introduction of the Buy to Let scheme in 1996. Before this date it was not possible to rent out mortgaged property, at least not without the express permission of the mortgage lender. High-interest bank loans were the only means of raising revenue for investment properties. But now it has become possible to obtain a mortgage especially devised for the investment landlord, and related only to property not intended as a personal home.

This scheme, which has proved extremely successful, has brought a new type of landlord into being: the middle-class small investor who is neither grasping nor greedy, but who wants to do something more interesting and tangible with some spare money than putting it into pension schemes, stocks and shares.

Buy-to-let investors in the UK rent out 70% of their properties to young professionals. There is growing evidence to suggest that the young and affluent are renting more now than in the past. It used to be that people would rent because they could not afford to buy. Now more people choose to rent because they want to. There are lots of reasons why this is happening. For example, the average age of first time buyers has increased, which may mean they are renting for longer before committing to a mortgage themselves. More people move around with their jobs and there are more single occupancy households. All of these people still want a nice place to call home, but don't necessarily want to be tied to a particular property.

Because they are very often high-earning professionals, or at least used to a good lifestyle, the new renters are extremely fussy, and demand is now for high-quality rental properties, not dismal, damp, dilapidated places with stained carpets, miserable wallpaper and poor furniture.

There are many ways of being a landlord today in the UK and each one has its own pros and cons. And if the service of providing others with rented accommodation is no longer an automatic licence to print money, those who are successful can do very nicely indeed. During 2002, 79% of buy-to-let borrowers stated they would consider adding to their property portfolio, with 64% stating that they would ideally like between two and ten properties. Of the entire buy-to-let properties, 39% are flats, 32% terraced houses, 20% semi-detached houses, 6% detached houses and only 3% bungalows.

TOP TIPS FOR UK BUY TO LET SUCCESS

◆ Do your homework. Make sure you know which type of property will let well. Remember it is not always the most expensive properties that give the best returns. It all depends on local demand.

◆ Do your sums. Think about how much you can afford to invest, work out how much your monthly mortgage repayment will be. Rental income should cover at least 125% of the monthly mortgage payment.

◆ Do speak to the right people. For example, letting agents can give some idea of the type of properties that are renting well in any particular area and can also offer help by giving a general indication of rent levels.

◆ Do ensure you budget for ongoing costs. These will include maintenance, the cost of repairing or replacing fixtures and fittings and buildings insurance.

◆ Do think of buy-to-let as a long-term investment. There will be no 'get rich quick' rewards, but you will have an additional property at the end of it all.

◆ Do budget for void periods between lettings, where you do not have any tenants and therefore no rental income.

◆ Do not underestimate the initial cost of your investment. As well as the deposit, you will need to cover solicitors' fees and other typical home buying costs.

◆ Do not ignore the fact that you will be running your own business and as such will need to adhere to certain legal and financial requirements.

◆ Do not rush into anything.

BUY TO LET ABROAD

It has long been a dream of many Britons to buy a place in the sun in which to rest and relax, and maybe retire. And a part of that dream can be the prospect of making the place pay for itself by letting it to others when not occupying it yourself. But buying a place in the sun can be rather like trying to make a holiday romance permanent. What works wonderfully well for two weeks, when relaxed, happy, stress-free and optimistic, may not look so good when it is turned into a lasting relationship.

When thinking about a buy-to-let property abroad take into account the same considerations as buying investment property in the UK. The mix will however be different. There will be unusual types of property, a sunny climate, exotic locations and a different type of tenant. People abroad are accustomed to renting. In some parts of Europe over 40% still rent their homes compared to just 11% in the UK.

There has been no shift in Spanish legislation allowing mortgage lenders to advance sums of money for buy-to-let properties. Personal finance for multiple properties is still through expensive bank loans. Why? The market in Spain is in equilibrium; in some case the competition in holiday resorts is so fierce it is driving rental prices downwards.

Do not forget that the customs, laws and traditions of Spain are very different from those back home. The buying procedures, banking arrangements and taxation, to name but a few, are all different. If the property needs alteration or renovation local workmen, who have their own distinctive ways, will do it. When letting a property it is important to take into account Spanish laws that can unwittingly trap the unwary.

CASE STUDY – CITY CENTRE APARTMENT

Alicante is cosmopolitan. Rents are high. Property prices are relatively low. It is a regional Spanish capital, and an excellent communications hub with Spain's busiest regional airport nearby. A true Spanish city, it sits at the heart of an international playground called the Costa Blanca. It is a major business and commercial centre, too. Alicante's main feature is the well-preserved Castillo de Santa Barbara, rising high over the city on its rocky base. The views from its battlements are stunning, taking in a vast panorama often reaching to the Balearic Islands. Benidorm, with its non-stop nightlife, is close by but Alicante has beaches too, and it can party. However its bonfire fiestas, the *Hogueras*, are a more traditional celebration.

The story began when Heather surprisingly inherited a sum of money. Not enough to buy a house in Brighton where she lived, but too much to blow away on a holiday, more clothes and an overdraft reduction. So the net result was the purchase of a city centre flat in Alicante that could be rented out for part of the year, and used personally for the rest of the time.

'Don't go to Madrid, it's too hot, Barcelona is nice but expensive, flights to Sevilla are infrequent'. Advice was forthcoming from all directions. 'Go for the Med, a good climate, lots of things going on. Don't look at a fourth-floor flat if there is no lift. Nobody has car parking, so don't worry about that. Floors should all be tiled. Avoid anything that needs decoration.'

Heather started by doing an Internet search to find out what was available, where and at what price. From this the ideal apartment was defined – city centre, one bedroom, 50 square metres, about 125,000 euros. A few mouse clicks later three estate agents were given the task of finding a Buy to Let flat for Fun and Profit.

A few weeks later she went to Alicante. On the appointed day, at the set time plus 30 minutes she met the moustached Pedro who marched her off to her first viewing. It was an apartment in a triangular skyscraper halfway between the old city centre and a new shopping mall. It had a room with a sink and bits of wire sticking out of the wall where light fittings should be, the bathroom had fungus and a 1995 newspaper covered dampness in the living area. 'Senora, you don't like it then?' said Pedro. 'Perhaps we go look at an other one?'

Apartment number two was slightly better. It had a good location around the walls of Castillo de Santa Barbara but was probably built at the same time and was definitely due for renovation. 'No? You will like the next one,' said Pedro 'in the meantime lets go for a *café con leche* and a croissant'.

A few streets back from the seafront and close to major shops and parks, Alicante's life can be found. Shops, parks, pedestrian areas, restaurants, pavement cafes, fast food joints and nightlife too. Do potential business renters object to overlooking shops and cafes, or does it offer value added accommodation? Let's hope for the latter, because the flat was just right. On the third floor, in a block of apartments, quiet, two rooms, tiled floors, even more tiles in the bathroom, a large kitchen and 64 square metres. The bonus – it was truly Spanish!

So that was it! Pedro's moustache bristled with pride. Another sale, another fee. A 10% deposit was required. The contract was signed. Completion of the purchase was in a few weeks. Allow another 10% for legal fees. A small Euro mortgage would be required from a Spanish bank – and that was put in the contract in case of delays.

She enjoyed her new flat. Brighton to Alicante was only two and a half hours away. Flights from Gatwick were daily and numerous. Low cost airlines, last minute bookings on charter flights and scheduled flights were all available. After a few months she signed up with a rental agency. Business and corporate clients only, three to four months maximum, was the tenant specification.

The rental agency collects the rents, organises repair and maintenance, finds tenants and arranges the utility payments. The flat is equipped with standard fixtures and fittings plus a television, video and a washer/dryer. Heather now has a Spanish bank account to pay the mortgage, receive the rent and pay any non-housekeeping bills – all in Euros. This keeps the accounting easy and avoids exchange rate fluctuations. Of course there are taxes to pay, sometime, somewhere, but there is also *mañana*...

TOP TIPS FOR BUY TO LET SUCCESS ABROAD

◆ It is important that the general location should have been visited on a few occasions since there is no substitute for first-hand knowledge.

◆ Consider whether the property is served by an adequate infrastructure, such as airport, roads, utility supplies, shops and medical facilities.

◆ Should the property be a villa, chalet or apartment? Should it be coastal or inland, in a busy location or secluded?

◆ Consider the amount of personal occupancy and what happens to the property when not lived in.

◆ What is the attraction of the property in the eyes of the tenant? Is there a tenant market for the property?

◆ Consider if there is someone locally who can be relied upon to manage the property. If not, consider engaging the services of a local management agent. Consider what the costs are in each case.

◆ What funding is required? Can the property be bought for cash? If not it may be appropriate to take out a loan.

SUMMARY

◆ Becoming a landlord requires skills. The foremost is a commitment to property.

◆ Even today there is a stigma associated with being a landlord.

◆ The buy-to-let market in the UK is expanding rapidly

fuelled by changes in social patterns and an alteration to the UK mortgage lending laws.

◆ There have been successive and parallel changes in rental laws in both the UK and Spain. The rental market in both countries is now considered to be in equilibrium.

◆ The new landlord is young and upwardly mobile. So are the tenants.

◆ Buy-to-let abroad has the same characteristics as the UK market – with sun and local customs.

◆ A top tip for letting abroad, in fact three top tips – location, location and location.

$$\boxed{3}$$

Knowing the Marketplace

THINKING STRATEGY

If intending to invest substantial sums buying and then renting a property in Spain it is absolutely necessary to get it right. Time consuming though it is, a thorough understanding of the marketplace is essential and this work will pay dividends later. Like all good business propositions let us start by writing a strategic statement.

Against a background of the worldwide economic situation and Spain's natural advantages, buy-to-let investors offer to supply different types of homes in various locations to the letting marketplace with each seeking to maintain a position of competitive advantage. The demand for rental property is from visitors and residents of all nationalities, including Spaniards themselves, at work, rest, or play looking for properties that give easy access to desirable features or entertainment, supported by a multimillion Euro advertising and promotion budget from the Spanish Tourist Board.

FOLLOW LONDON

During recessions people will take fewer overseas holidays and property prices will be deflated. In times of relative prosperity more people will take overseas holidays and property prices will increase. A depressed worldwide economy sends out a property buy signal that should be timed to the best advantage when the economy begins to swing upwards. Conversely a buoyant economy stimulates the housing market and raises the possibility of selling at its peak. All this simply means the buy-to-let investors have to get their purchase timing correct for their own personal financial circumstances.

Property prices vary nationally. The UK has one of the highest price structures in Europe and the south east of England is recognised as the most expensive area, with London hitting a peak. A good guide is to follow London. Changes in the housing market often start in London and the south east and ripple outwards to the rest of the UK. What happens in London is a reflection of what is happening to the USA economy, for the UK is a follower and not a leader in world economics. Following London can give advance warning of coming changes.

An annual publication by London Residential Research is aimed at developers and agents. However, an average amateur buy-to-let person will find it extremely instructive. It monitors new developments in every residential area in London, publishing prices, yields, which districts are going up and which are going down.

It does not claim to have all the answers but no sensible developer ignores the trends, statistics and issues highlighted since it is possible to recognise various projects that are considered a good investment. Investment is not risk free and it may be that a heavily geared landlord will discover that interest rates will be a couple of points ahead of rental returns, but the bottom line is that a decent London flat will not do an Enron, Marconi or Railtrack.

The publication demonstrates different ambitions in the property market. It can help focus on whether to buy off-plan and double your money by selling on in 18 months time, or invest in something that gives a little bit of income and then a lot of capital growth, or even an investment with no cash flow now but a thumping great payout after 20 years.

What relevance does this have to buy-to-let for fun and profit in Spain? Directly none. Indirectly it is very useful to read, to understand the complexities of the property market and the terminology used. It is a source of information, an increase in knowledge.

SPAIN'S NATURAL ADVANTAGES
There is no question the overwhelming attraction of Spain is its wonderful climate. Climate is the big, big number

one. It is healthy, makes one feel good and equally importantly encourages people to enjoy life to the full. While northern Europe is being deluged with rain and battered by wind, with roads closed by snow, and ice affecting transport, you can almost guarantee that Alicante and Malaga will be bathed in sunshine (see Figure 4).

The influences of the Mediterranean and Atlantic produce a wide range of climatic conditions. Summers everywhere are hot. Spring and autumn are wonderfully pleasant. In winter the Costas and the Islands are mild, but the north west and, surprisingly, the interior can go below freezing.

A good climate has to be a balance. Not too hot, not too cold, a little bit of rain to grow the crops, but not too much to deter people. Some snow in the mountains for recreational purposes but not enough to affect communications. Northern Spain has its lush green pastures. The Costas offer sun and sand coupled with the clear blue waters of the Mediterranean. The southern rolling hills of Andalucia attract little movement in the blistering summer heat. The Balearic and Canary Islands are always pleasant. Madrid, the capital, is either freezing or roasting.

A second advantage of Spain is the low cost of living. But Spain is no longer the cheap and cheerful country it once was. The cost of living has increased considerably over the last decade. However, with the exception of the large cities, the cost of living is still lower in coastal and rural

		Jan	Feb	Mar	Apr	May	Jun	Jul	Aug	Sep	Oct	Nov	Dec
Costa Brava	Max	14	14	16	17	20	23	27	26	25	21	16	15
	Min	6	6	8	9	12	16	18	21	17	13	9	7
Costa Dorado	Max	13	14	16	18	21	25	28	28	25	21	16	13
	Min	6	7	9	11	14	18	21	21	19	15	11	8
Costa del Azahar	Max	15	16	18	20	23	26	29	29	27	23	19	16
	Min	6	6	8	10	13	16	19	20	18	15	10	7
Costa Blanca	Max	16	18	20	22	26	29	32	32	30	25	21	17
	Min	7	6	8	10	13	15	19	20	18	15	10	7
Costa Calida	Max	15	16	18	19	23	25	29	29	27	24	20	17
	Min	5	5	8	9	13	17	20	20	18	14	10	7
Costa del Sol	Max	17	17	19	21	23	27	29	30	29	23	20	17
	Min	9	9	11	13	15	19	21	22	20	16	12	9
Costa de la Luz	Max	15	14	18	21	23	27	29	30	29	23	20	17
	Min	8	7	11	12	15	18	20	20	19	15	12	9
Santander	Max	12	12	15	15	17	19	22	22	21	18	15	12
	Min	7	7	8	10	11	14	16	18	15	12	10	8
Galicia	Max	14	15	16	18	20	24	25	26	24	20	16	14
	Min	3	4	5	7	10	12	13	13	12	9	6	5
Sevilla	Max	15	17	21	23	26	32	35	36	32	26	20	16
	Min	6	6	9	11	13	17	21	20	18	14	10	7
Balearic Islands	Max	14	15	17	19	22	26	29	29	27	23	18	15
	Min	6	6	8	10	13	17	19	20	18	14	11	8
Canary Islands East	Max	21	21	22	23	23	24	25	26	26	27	24	22
	Min	16	16	16	17	18	19	21	22	22	21	18	17
Canary Islands West	Max	20	21	22	23	24	26	28	29	28	26	24	21
	Min	14	14	15	16	17	19	20	21	21	19	17	16
Madrid	Max	9	11	15	18	21	27	31	30	25	19	13	9
	Min	1	2	5	12	10	14	17	17	14	10	5	2

Figure 4. Temperature (degrees centigrade).

areas than it is in the United Kingdom, Ireland, Germany and France. It is significantly lower than the cost of living in the Scandinavian countries and is on a par with Florida.

Returning to the major advantage of climate, it has to be emphasised that the seasons magnify or hide some of Spain's more interesting characteristics. The need to see an area in all seasons cannot be over emphasised. Some summer resorts close down almost completely in the winter months, and a climate which is so agreeable in June can be drab in January. Conversely, somewhere that was a tranquil 20 minute drive from town in May might be accessible only with a two hour, nose to tail driving ordeal in August.

Spring
Spring is time for renewal. Flowers bud and fill the air with a crisp clean fragrance. Peace, harmony and tranquillity are just a few of the splendours found in Spain. The countryside is at its best as wild flowers bloom before the onset of the summer heat. Water flows to crops giving a green look to a sometimes barren landscape. Blankets of wildflowers dot the landscape with blues, purples, yellows and other colours of the rainbow.

Life in Spain moves outdoors with the arrival of spring. Cafes fill with people. This is a good time to look at Spain. Everything is fresh and clean. The summer crowds are absent. Spring brings the emerging warm sunshine. Layers of clothing will soon be peeled off as the weeks progress.

Summer

August is Spain's big holiday season. Madrid empties as Spaniards flock to the coast or to the mountains to escape the searing heat of the interior. Their numbers are swelled by millions of foreign tourists. Entertainment and eating only takes place in the cool of the evening, when the temperature drops. In the summer fiestas are everywhere. But it is hot, it is stifling and there are too many people.

It is possible to adventure in the cooler mountains in some of the most beautiful places on earth. Mountain biking, hiking, golf, fishing or riding a horse can be a radical alternative to simply lying on the beach. Whatever activities – it is possible to enjoy them in Spain.

White cotton clothing to deflect the sun, cool footwear and a hat, together with lots of t-shirts and shorts for leisurewear, are all that is required for a Spanish summer.

Autumn

After the heat of summer, before the rainy season, the countryside, roads and properties have a dirty, unwashed and unattractive appearance as a thin film of dust covers the landscape. In the country trees show off their glorious colours in welcoming winter and bidding farewell to summer. Spectacular colours adorn the countryside with fauna and flora changing the hillsides from brown to green.

Towards the end of this quarter the rain arrives, sometimes heavy torrential rain. The northern tourist resorts practically close down. But the harvesting of crops continues, with grape and wine production taking over as the main cultural and agricultural event. The hunting season begins.

The days are still warm, the nights cool and, in the mountains, crisp. The climate is pleasant during this season but a sweater is advisable due to temperatures dropping in the evening. Expect clear blue skies and twinkling stars.

Winter

It is often said that winter is a good time to look at Spain. The other side of the coin is seen as urbanisations empty, many restaurants close, and coastal resorts appear quite desolate. Winter does vary greatly from region to region. Snowfalls bring skiers to the slopes, while in the lower areas olives, oranges and lemons are gathered. The cold of Madrid contrasts with the warmth of the Canaries' high tourist season.

It is possible to sunbathe in sheltered spots in the winter but January, February and even March can all be wet, cold and miserable. As you sit by the roaring fire you can also watch the snow fall on the high mountains of the Sierra Nevada. Winter in Spain brings excitement, fun and adventure. Christmas is a special time for family reunions, giving presents, sharing food and attending religious celebrations.

Acclimatising

When visitors and new residents from northern Europe first come to Spain they find the summers very hot. They sweat profusely and often feel tired and lethargic. In winter they are comfortable but surprised to see Spaniards wrapped up heavily with coats and scarves.

After two years living in the country they acclimatise. The shorts worn in autumn and spring are replaced with long trousers. Summer is comfortable. Winter is cold. If they go back to Germany, Scandinavia or the UK, they freeze. The climate has not changed, but the individual has acclimatised.

WHO SUPPLIES THE MARKETPLACE?

The vast majority of available Spanish lettings are from people who have bought homes according to their needs – size, price and location. They have bought holiday homes and are not so much looking to make a profit from renting as hoping to cover some or all of the costs of purchase through rental income by letting them casually to family and friends. They are holiday homes for their own use, and they will be ready to compromise on the business issues thus reducing potential income in order to maximise their own enjoyment.

A smaller number of people see property exclusively as an investment proposition and want to rent out on a serious basis. They want to make money by letting their property and will try to find the maximum number of tenants each year. The decisions they take about where and what to buy and what facilities to provide will be governed by a wish to maximise profit. They put themselves in the position of the person who may wish to rent their property and consider which part of the market they expect to appeal to; whether it is couples wanting to enjoy rural Spain, families wanting a traditional beach holiday or groups on a golfing break. They choose an area, a location, buy a property and equip it solely with their prospective tenants in mind.

Lastly there is the new breed of people who Buy to Let for Fun and Profit. They seek a balance between casual letting and serious letting. They want to enjoy the property and make money too!

Figure 5 highlights combinations within the rental market-place.

CASE STUDY – CURING ILLS

Mark suffered from arthritis. He had been advised several times that living in a warm climate would be of some benefit to his condition. On visits to Spain, talking to fellow sufferers he confirmed this to be true. Mark and his wife Jill had strong social ties with the rugby set in Bath. Nearing retirement they decided they would purchase an additional property in Spain, spending the summers in Bath and the winters in Spain.

In order to avoid the thousands of holidaymakers they decided to purchase a property away from the coast, a few kilometres inland in a village called Orba with a strong English community. When they were not in Spain the property would be rented out to defray some of their expenses.

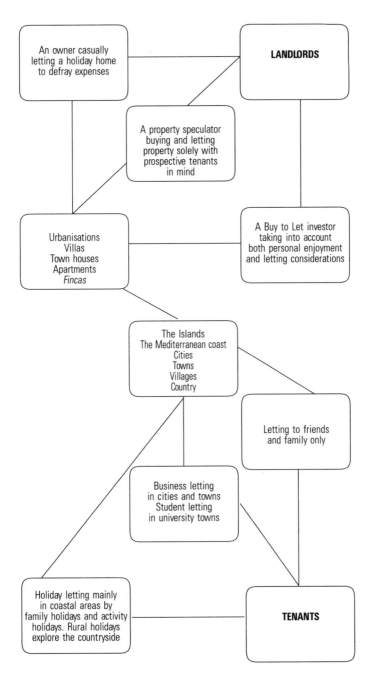

Figure 5. Property rental marketing mix.

SELECTING THE RIGHT LOCATION

The key to a successful rental property is definitely its location. It is by far the most important decision to be made. Location will also be a major factor in the price paid for a property directly impacting on occupancy rates and income. A villa around a golf course will cost far more than an apartment inland. On the other hand, it will also be more sought after as a letting proposition and will command a higher rental. Like so many other things getting the location right is a balance between what can be afforded and the potential income to be generated.

Although it is possible to choose a region of Spain that is attractive, deciding on a particular town, village, development or hillside to purchase a property for personal use and also to let out involves a whole series of much more individual, more commercialised choices.

Most people know within a few minutes of arriving in a town whether it is somewhere they like or not. But to underline a recurring theme – there is a need to think differently about the location of a property depending on whether it is just a place to spend leisure time, or if intending to live there permanently or if the property is to be let out in the owner's absence. These differing sets of considerations can potentially limit a purchasing choice.

Age comes into it too! A spectacular mountain track that provides the only access to a restored farmhouse may seem an attraction when in full health, but is not so good when driving up and down it every time to visit the shops 20 years later. Access to public transport and medical services will become more important too, and the closeness of other ex-pats, who were avoided in earlier years, may become more comforting.

However, initially a buy-to-let for fun and profit is about getting it right for the owner. So there is a need to be very clear about the owner's requirements. Some basic questions have to be asked. They concern location – where to go.

♦ How far away from the summer crowd do you really want to be? Tourist towns can become massively crowded. If you do not want this, look away from the beach and go inland. Most people find a 30 minute drive convenient from a reasonably sized town.

♦ You may wish your property to be close to local shops, bars and restaurants, public transport, a good beach, golf and other sports facilities, arts and entertainment.

♦ Is the choice city, rural life or perhaps Green Spain?

♦ Do you seek a remote location? This can be a problem. Where are the nearest bus, coach and train services? How good are the roads? How easy is it to connect to the motorway network?

♦ How many of the local facilities stay open in the winter? This is particularly important if you are considering moving to a tourist area where there is a great difference between high and low season.

♦ Is being close to a beach and holiday entertainment important? If that's what you want then look no further than the Mediterranean Costas and the two groups of islands, the Balearics and the Canaries.

◆ How much sun do you need? For reliable mainland sunshine stay south of Valencia or in the Canaries.

◆ How close to neighbours is an important issue because so many Spanish properties are in an apartment or on a high-density urbanisation. In some holiday home urbanisations no neighbours exist at all for long periods.

◆ How close do you really want to be to compatriots? There are British communities that allow their inhabitants to isolate themselves from every aspect of Spanish life other than a meal, a drink and a visit to a social club. On the other hand there are towns and villages just inland with smaller, more mixed, foreign communities.

◆ Do you have any special interests or hobbies in which you can take part in this location? What is the social life like in the area and will it suit you?

GETTING IT RIGHT FOR TENANTS

There will be an overlap between the requirements for the owner and the facilities for the tenants. But the key marketing question for tenants is, 'What is so unique about this property and why would they want to go there?'

At 40 million the population of Spain is less than many European countries. With 78 people per square kilometre it has one of the lowest population densities in Europe. 50 million people of all nationalities, but mainly British, visit

Spain each year. Given that the Spanish too take many breaks the potential holiday letting market is massive. On top of that there are business and student lets!

Buy-to-let investors would do well to consider a location which is supported by the latest trends in Spanish tourism. The Spanish Tourist Board backs promotional and advertising initiatives heavily and these, if successful, present opportunities that are considered by holiday tenants. There is much of interest in the country that can be commended to the discriminating tourist as well as sun, sea and sand and sporting activities. Visiting churches, cathedrals or museums, admiring the grandeur of towers, bridges or walls, or just walking along the streets are invitations to travel through history.

Appendix 5 gives details of attractions, many brash, some natural, where today's tourist is being encouraged to go.

Spanish tourist offices are excellent sources of information. They are well equipped with publications and information. Offices exist in cities, towns, and airports or near beauty spots. One very quick and effective method of obtaining information on activities and places of interest is simply to click on to each *Comunidad*'s web page. Everything you could possibly want to know about a region is instantly available – in English, worldwide, before you even leave home. Appendix 11 has a list of useful websites.

It is helpful to build up a profile of the type of person to rent a property. There may be more than one profile for a property, for example a holiday let and a business let in a Mediterranean city. It may be local people or people from overseas. It may embrace families with children, business-men, professional or retired couples. Picture these profiles. Marketing is all about understanding what the customer wants and then providing it.

SEEKING COMPETITIVE ADVANTAGE

Competitive advantage should be considered at two levels. Firstly, in comparing one location to another and secondly within a chosen location. For example, does a Buy to Let in the Picos offer a better competitive position than one in the Alpujarras? Secondly, if the location in the Picos is chosen what distinguishes this property from any other on offer? Unfortunately when it comes to letting Spanish properties there are often two stark choices, which have to be avoided. A remote, cheap, hard-to-reach property will be difficult to let, and conversely an expensive property in an already popular tourist area will face intense competition from other rental properties.

In the latter case the property will be hard to let if it is vastly more expensive or less well equipped than similar properties in the area. It is important to ensure that an apartment or villa is not inferior in any way to others in the same area. For instance, if all the villas in the area have private swimming pools, then one without may not attract many paying customers. In extremely popular tourist areas there will also be competition from interna-tional holiday companies who are in a position to offer discounts on holiday packages.

Before making a buying commitment, contact letting agents in the locality as they can give a view on the letting potential of a property. Competitors are also one of the best sources of information. Understand the standard offering, what the successful operators are doing well and what less successful operators are doing wrong. All the time, look for ideas and think about what point of difference can be created in letting and how to improve on the standard offering.

SUMMARY

◆ It is important to understand the strategic nature of Spain's letting market.

◆ Before buying, ensure that the worldwide economic signals are favourable. Consider the trends coming from London.

◆ Spain's natural advantages are its excellent climate and low cost of living. But beware as seasonal changes can disguise some important facts.

◆ Currently, people rent out their holiday homes and professional full-time landlords supply the letting market. Buy to Let for Fun and Profit is a new, high potential concept for Spain.

◆ Selecting the right location for both the owner and tenants is the number one issue to be considered. But getting it right for the owner is the first consideration.

◆ Tenants will be strongly influenced by the promotion and advertising undertaken by the Spanish Tourist Board.

◆ Always seek competitive advantage.

4

Keying into Mobility

While knowing the marketplace is one aspect of successful letting, understanding the mobility of people within that market is another more complicated social issue. Underlined already are the two principal reasons for going to or living in Spain, which are the excellent climate and lower cost of living. But there are other issues!

Northern Europeans move to Spain to work, rest or play. Or to put it another way, they go on holiday, they are Spain's new residents (permanent, temporary, declared, undeclared, full-time or part-time) or they go for employment purposes. Spaniards too move for work, rest and play but in different proportions to their northern neighbours.

Understanding these issues plays an important part in determining a tenant market. People on the move are letting opportunities. They all need a roof over their heads, albeit a temporary one.

GOING ON HOLIDAY FROM NORTHERN EUROPE

Most Europeans obtain direct experience of foreign countries from tourism. Since the 1960s, there has been remarkable growth in foreign holidays. This has been fuelled by reductions in real prices and the increased understanding of foreign holidays as 'positional goods'. The two dominant nationalities of European holiday-makers come from the UK and Germany. In 1965 the number of British people going abroad was 5 million: the number increased by 140% by 1980 and doubled again by 1995. Equally impressive are the statistics for the proportion of the UK population taking a holiday abroad – 13% in 1971 and 35% in 1995. Well over half the British population has taken a foreign vacation at some time. Those who holiday abroad tend to be younger, more prosperous and of higher socio-economic status than those who holiday in Britain. The growth in international tourism from Germany has been even more rapid. Whereas only 5.8 million went abroad in 1962, this rose to 18.3 million in 1985 and to 40.7 million in 1995 (partly boosted by reunification).

Not all holidaying is by mass tourists. There are many types of tourists seeking a different experience from their travels. Tourists seek both novelty and familiarity. There are four types:

- The organised mass tourist, who takes an inclusive holiday which offers protection within an environmental bubble. Familiarity dominates over novelty.

- The individual mass tourist who is more autonomous and follows a flexible itinerary. Familiarity dominates but some novelty is sought.

- The explorer investigates new areas and tries to get off the beaten track. Novelty is sought but if it becomes stressful, this tourist will retreat into the familiarity of the environmental bubble.

- The back to nature drifter, who avoids any kind of commercial tourism establishment, seeks contact with native culture and tries to live the same way as locals.

One other relevant feature has been the growth of winter sun holidays. Some 12 million British holiday visits are made between October and March each year to various overseas locations. In general, overseas winter holidays have been expanding at about twice the rate of summer sun holidays. Older people constitute an important element of this market, with 23% aged 55 and over. There have also been other changes in the Mediterranean tourism market, notably an increase in self-catering that can sometimes be the first step towards later retirement. The experience of renting a villa or apartment may lead to the purchase of a holiday home with some of these later used for retirement.

The traditional Spanish package holiday, still enjoyed by many, consists of sand, sea and sun. Holiday reps efficiently escort people from the airport to a three or four star hotel with half board accommodation, offer trips and sort out any problems. The tourists stay in their self-imposed environmental bubble. This type of holiday will always be the core of Spain's tourist industry but it has now peaked. It has spawned a massive expenditure to keep its visitors happy and to encourage them to visit again and again.

The Spanish holiday market is now segmented: firstly into different types of accommodation such as hotels, time-shares, rented properties and holiday homes; secondly into the traditional family holiday; thirdly into special interest groups looking for cultural, rural, walking, sporting or adventure holidays and fourthly to encourage tourists away from the Costa's to rural inland areas. To do this the Spanish Tourist Board has developed a number of concepts which can be seen in national newspaper and TV advertising and in promotional literature:

- Traditional sun, sea and sand.

- Espana Verde (Green Spain) covering the northern regions of the country embracing Asturias, Galicia, Cantabria and Pais Vasco.

- The Gold and Silver routes that are old Roman roads through the Spanish heartland.

- There are over 700 Heritage of Mankind sites world-wide declared by UNESCO. Spain has just eight Spanish cities recognised for their artistic and cultural legacy. They are Avila, Caceres, Cordoba, Cuenca,

Salamanca, Santiago de Compostela, Segovia and Toledo. They are not major cultural cities such as Granada, but smaller, more rural cities each with a wealth of history and culture, a variety of customs and delicious cuisine.

◆ Short city breaks are promoted to Alicante, Barcelona, Madrid, Palma, Salamanca, Santander, Santiago de Compostela, Sevilla, Toledo, and Valencia.

The buy-to-let investor will also need to look at future tourism trends as well as past performance. Expanding trends that may impact on future letting business include:

◆ The growth in short breaks and out-of-season holidays.

◆ The growth in activity-based and learning holidays.

◆ The growth in the retirement market.

◆ The growing awareness of environmental issues.

◆ A trend towards a continuous improvement in the facilities offered.

◆ The rapid increase in bookings via the Internet.

NEW FOREIGN RESIDENTS

While most of Spain's visitors are transient, some northern Europeans become permanent residents mainly near the Mediterranean and the Islands. The early trickle of migrants has become a steady flow, forming one of the principal international retirement locations originating from northern Europe. For this group of people climate is important but another reason is grounded in personal finances, as there are considerable house price differentials between northern and southern Europe. A full list of reasons why people may wish to move permanently to Spain are:

◆ Climate and other aspects of the natural environment such as landscape and clean air.

◆ The pace of life, feeling healthier and more relaxed, opportunities for golf, sailing and active sports.

◆ Lower living costs, housing costs, cheaper food, less heating bills and lower taxes.

◆ The presence of a British community, many friends, a good social life, the opportunity for relatives to visit, and a friendly local population.

◆ Admiration for Spain, the country's society and culture.

◆ Childhood or family links, including marriage to a Spaniard.

◆ Antipathy to the UK, such as high crime or poor social values, a general wish to live abroad or long-term expatriates with no wish to return to the UK.

◆ English is widely spoken, easy travel to UK.

◆ Work or business links to Spain before retirement.

Figures 6 and 7 quantify the reasons why British people chose to live permanently in Spain together with some of the downsides. Some reasons are based on the climate, attractions that are shared in large measure with tourism, which also generates some of the infrastructure and social requirements of those who move here permanently.

Climate and environment	48.1%
Pace of life and health	18.4%
Childhood, family links	8.9%
Antipathy to the UK	8.9%
Lower living costs	6.2%
Admiration of Spain	5.0%
Work or business	2.7%
Social advantages	2.1%
Practical advantages	1.8%

Figure 6. Reasons for residing in Spain (Source: *Sunset Lives*).

Language difficulties	34.3%
Separated from family	17.9%
Other reasons	13.5%
Bureaucracy and red tape	12.1%
Lack of mental stimulation	7.9%
Exchange rate/banking difficulties	6.4%
Rising cost of living	3.6%
Poor medical/hospital facilities	3.2%
Cost of air travel	1.1%

Figure 7. Disadvantages of living in Spain (Source: *Sunset Lives*).

There are 250,000 ex-pats along the 120 kilometre stretch of the Costa del Sol, with perhaps an even larger population along the Costa Blanca and as many as 100,000 who have made it to the Balearics Islands. With a further 30% 'permanent' holidaymakers you have an expat community rapidly approaching a million. These statistics are approximate as a large percentage of people who own property do not reside full-time in Spain and there is an additional grouping of those who reside, but choose not to declare their presence in the country for tax purposes.

In the new millennium, who is actually buying property? About 70% of the total market is British, with around 35% in the over-55 bracket. Taking all nationalities into account the over-55s make up around 50% of the total market. There is a large demand in the Costa Blanca from the Irish. Germans, who for a long period dominated the purchasing scene, are in decline as high taxation back home has affected their disposable income. Transparency between the German and Spanish tax authorities has also resulted in many selling their properties, which can no longer be regarded as tax-free.

Of the three key destinations, the Costa del Sol, Costa Blanca and the Balearics, it is the Costa Blanca that rates as the main retirement destination. This is largely to do with the fact that it is cheaper than the other two areas and has attracted people who have a modest disposable income compared to more wealthy people who invested in property when they were in their 40s. Both Menorca and Mallorca have large retirement communities, established in the days before property prices went sky high.

A permanent resident is required to register his presence at the local Town Hall. He or she is then on the voting register, the only true population record and effectively an official census. Looking at registered voters statistics closely, the Costa Blanca (Alicante Province) has the greatest number of foreign residents (21%) with the British the largest grouping. The popularity of the overdeveloped Costa del Sol is declining. The Irish tiger economy has seen their numbers swell and there has been a large influx of people from Eastern block countries as the EU expanded.

Figures 8, 9 and 10 are the official statistics. But of course not all towns, cities and communities reflect the overall trend. Mallorca still has an overwhelmingly strong German presence. So too do Calpe and Denia. The figures for Barcelona and Madrid reflect government, business and educational interests. Inland and in the north of Spain, there is little penetration of foreign voters.

Area	Number
Alicante Province	108,193
Malaga	64,548
Balerics	50,311
Tenerife	43,894
Barcelona	39,601
Madrid	37,488
Las Palmas	25,987
Valencia	13,277
Murcia	7,076

Figure 8. Location of registered non-Spanish voters.

Country	Number
UK	131,675
Germany	115,440
France	57,984
Portugal	57,838
Italy	57,711
Netherlands	27,200
Ireland	5,389

Figure 9. Nationality of registered non-Spanish voters.

Country	Number
UK	41,521
Germany	27,271
Netherlands	9,766
Belgium	7,933
France	6,876
Norway	5,336
Sweden	4,362
Italy	3,343
Finland	1,594
Ireland	1,064

Figure 10. Nationality of registered non-Spanish voters on the
Costa Blanca (21% of all citizens with voting rights).

CASE STUDY – OVER THE GREEN

If there is such a thing as a cautious adventurer it was Jim
McCloud. He and his family had been looking for a
Spanish property for four years, to be used eventually for
full- or part-time retirement but with good letting

potential in the interim. They enjoyed the only relatively concrete-free part of the Costa del Sol between Estepona and Gibraltar and in particular Sotogrande, a new development embracing a marina and a championship golf course.

But it was San Roque, close by, between Gibraltar and Algeciras that finally caught their attention. They went several times to stay in a hotel on the development to check out the property scene. 'I admit I am cautious by nature but I have to get this one correct' said Jim, a 53-year-old solicitor from Glasgow. He was interested in plans to build 15 detached houses, each with a swimming pool, facing the fairways of the well-known golf course, only 500 metres from a hotel and health spa and within 'a good drive' of the many shopping facilities.

Having seen the site and house plans, Jim decided the location had excellent letting potential, and put down a 10% deposit on a 500,000€ house with three bedrooms, two bathrooms, a stupendous living room and numerous terraces. Despite buying off-plan the home was completed on time, which is unusual for Spanish builders.

Their 'life plan' is working well. Jim and his family spend two months a year in their new home. It is let out part of the time during major golf championships and to other short-term tenants. In a few years time the family plan will change. They will move there full-time. It will be their permanent home.

GETTING EMPLOYMENT

Some people go to Spain to work or for an extended holiday. Casual or seasonal work is ideal for someone who has not firmed up a long-term life plan or is seeking to earn a few Euros while enjoying a life in the sun. It can be easy to get carried away by the seemingly casual lifestyle, the laid-back approach and amicable business methods, but these disguise a profit motive and it should not be assumed that working for an English-speaking northern European is better, because Spain is full of ex-pats who for one reason or another have decided to make a fragile living through running a bar, a shop or property dealing.

For professional people going to Spain to work, the most important requirement is an ability to speak good Spanish. The dominance of regional languages and dialects causes problems for foreigners and Spaniards from other parts of Spain but if seeking professional employment, learn the language. *Castillano* or a regional variation is the only option.

People who are fluent in Spanish and English can find work in the major cities as translators and interpreters where the task involves business correspondence or assisting northern Europeans with Spanish paperwork, or even at police stations on busy market days where petty theft is common and an interpreter is necessary.

For residents of Spain the chances of finding teaching work are considerably better than any other profession. Teaching English is big business. The Spanish wish to have a second language. For commercial reasons it has to be English. There is a constant demand for qualified teachers who can find a job quite easily. Where demand outstrips supply in the big cities a graduate native English speaker can get a job without other qualifications.

There are no restrictions on any class of employment. Members of EU countries are treated equally with Spanish nationals.

COMPARING SPANISH MOBILITY

The Spanish also work, rest and play. It is, however, their home where they have more options, greater opportunity, but less disposable income than most northern Europeans.

The holiday market for Spanish nationals is considerably smaller than the holiday market for foreign visitors. While 50 million foreign visitors fly in to enjoy a break in some form of accommodation, this does not mean that the entire 40 million population of Spain seeks similar relaxation. While it is true that many Spaniards flock from Madrid to the coast each August it is equally true to say that some stay at home, some go to other parts of Europe or America, some visit relatives, and some have holiday homes of their own.

The inescapable conclusion is that while holiday lettings are a big opportunity, they may be best targeted at foreign visitors. It does not mean that Spaniards do not play golf, ski or fish – of course they do, but in order for the Buy to Let investor to keep focused on the one big holiday tenant market they should aim at foreign visitors.

A similar picture emerges when exploring the retirement market. When foreigners first move to Spain they are advised to rent a property in an area before buying. This lessens the risk of getting it wrong. Spaniards do not have to do this. There is no letting market for Spaniards at retirement. They simply live in the same home, move back to their village or move to a place they know.

The employment market is quite the opposite. Northern Europeans seeking employment will predominantly be after casual work – except those in the teaching profession. The market for Spanish business lets is huge and the locations are easy to identify! Madrid and Barcelona are the top two cities with government and commercial people of all nationalities seeking rental property, quickly followed by the other Mediterranean cities of Valencia, Alicante and Malaga for Spanish nationals. There is a market for business lets in all Spanish towns but not all inland areas are attractive to a Buy to Let owner.

Students are also mainly Spanish nationals studying at key university towns such as Salamanca and Murcia, which are warmer versions of Oxford and Cambridge.

SUMMARY

◆ People on the move are all letting opportunities.

◆ People go to Spain to work, rest (retirement) or play (holiday).

◆ Holidaying in Spain is more sophisticated than simply mass tourism. It is segmented into differing types of accommodation, traditional holidays, green and rural issues, historical and cultural visits and short city breaks.

- The buy-to-let investor should look to future tourism trends as well as past statistics.

- Spain's new residents are mainly Britons aged over 55 years who come for many reasons in addition to climate and cost of living. The official Town Hall statistics do not reflect the overall numbers of foreigners.

- The holiday letting market is best targeted at northern Europeans.

- The business letting market is best targeted at Spanish nationals in major or provincial cities.

5

Deciding Where to Go

MAJOR COASTAL AREAS

The popularity of Spain's coastal areas is undiminished. The climate and amenities are at their best. Although heavily populated in the summer by visitors these areas are the traditional ground for foreign property purchasers and therefore have many letting opportunities.

Costa Blanca

This area is distinguished by its fine climate. The principal holiday resorts are Benidorm and Torrevieja. It has fine commercial centres at Valencia, Spain's third largest city; Alicante, the main city on the Costa Blanca; Cartagena, a former naval base and of course Murcia, a lively university city. Tucked away to the south is the almost unknown area called the Costa Calida and to the north the Costa del Azahar.

Close to the sea there are several scenic nature reserves – the freshwater lagoons of L'Albufera near Valencia, the saltpans of Torrevieja and the limestone crag of the Penya d'Ifach Calpe. Inland the mountains around Alcoi await discovery, but the green Jalon Valley is now a magnet for much redevelopment.

Having warmer winters than the Costa Brava, cheaper and less fashionable than the Costa del Sol, the Costa Blanca occupies a prime stretch of Mediterranean coastline with Alicante's airport and main line railway station a major communication hub. Long sandy beaches, in places lined with hotels and apartment blocks, are a feature of the area.

There are two parts to the Costa Blanca. The northern Costa Blanca called the Marina Alta is the prettiest part, with rocky coves backed by rugged green mountains around its main towns of Denia, Javea, Calpe and Altea. Benidorm dominates the central Costa Blanca. Europe's largest single resort has a historic image problem. Build on success they say... and they do, bigger, higher, each hotel more luxurious than the last.

The southern Costa Blanca, below Alicante, is known as the Marina Baja. It is now one of the fastest-growing areas in Spain for holiday homes. Anyone looking for property will invariably come across the town of Torrevieja and Orihuela Costa, the fastest expanding region in Europe where, since the mid 80s houses have been built at a prodigious rate. In the next five years new homes are to be built at the rate of 6,000 units per year. Selling these homes either for permanent residence, holiday, or to let, is a major marketing exercise with companies all over Europe competing with a portfolio of detached, semi-detached, terraced and apartment style properties. What is the attraction? Properties here are cheap, the climate excellent, and communications are good. The downside – in summer it is wall-to-wall with people. The beaches are packed, and the restaurants are full. In winter, the white urbanisations are mostly uninhabited. Since virtually everything here is so new, this is not an area to assimilate Spanish culture.

Costa del Sol and Andalucia

Andalucia is a large area extending across the south of the country incorporating the deserts of Almeria, the wetlands of Donana, the snow capped peaks of the Sierra Nevada and the beaches of the Costa del Sol. The inland cities of Granada, Cordoba and Sevilla share a rich Moorish heritage. There is of course more to Andalucia than just the Costa del Sol. The Costa de la Luz sits on the Atlantic side of the region and the Costa Tropical has sprung up as the coastal area of Granada province.

But it is the Costa del Sol that holds our attention. It may be one of the most overdeveloped strips of coastline in the world, but thanks to 300 days of sunshine per year this area of Spain is home to many. It hosts the jet set sophistication of Marbella, and over 30 golf courses lying just inland. There are many resorts aimed at the mass tourist market, but some of the older developments, just south of Malaga, have a tired, well-worn look, with planners now facing the difficult task of possible demolition in this now seedy area.

The highlight of the area is unquestionably Marbella, a stylish resort, with Puerto Banus, its ostentatious marina. Expensive shops, restaurants and glittering nightlife reflect the wealth of its inhabitants and visitors. Close behind is the up and coming Sotogrande, an exclusive resort of luxury villas with a marina and golf course. Estepona is quieter, not so built-up and not attached to the long concrete strip that unfortunately is a characteristic of this Costa. Nerja and Almunecar too are gleaming white modern towns, good examples of popular residential areas. Malaga is another fine city with a thriving port. Its new shopping centre presents an interesting blend of the old and the new.

There are other towns but it is best to give them a miss. Home to high-rise holiday hotels, perhaps less brash than they were, and now run down, adequately describes Torremolinos and Fuengirola.

A few miles inland from the coast at Malaga a different Spain opens up. It is called the Alpujarras with lots of greenery and many thousands of classical white houses covering the slopes of its rounded hills. Even small towns are cut into the contours of the landscape. For a person looking for something different, and wishing to blend into the lifestyle of Andalucia, then this is the place to be. This is the land of the *finca,* a country house surrounded by orange, lemon, olive and almond trees, possibly lacking in all mod cons, but well away from other humans. It is rural life ... where time is not important.

Some Andalucians choose to live in fortified hilltop towns now known as *pueblos blancos* (white towns) whitewashed in the Moorish tradition and today working agricultural villages. Ronda is the most well known.

The Balearics

Often associated with mass inexpensive tourism, these islands have something for everyone. For those turning their back on the bustle of coastal resorts with all their attractions, the countryside and old towns lie relatively undisturbed. The Balearics have white villages, wooded hills and caves. Mallorca, a culturally rich island, has mountains to go with the sea and shore. Each of the islands has its own character and climate and, away from the big resorts and foreign-owned enclaves, there are towns, untouched stretches of countryside and even shoreline.

These islands have more hotel beds than some countries. They have towns where property is 75% foreign-owned. But 40 years of tourism has now given rise to a need for change. The locals feel the dominance of tourism over local life has become too great. They wish to appeal to a more up-market tourist and away from the cheap package holiday image. So enter the regional government's tourist tax to get tourists to pay more towards local conservation projects and amenities together with a series of local measures aimed at halting the cycle of uncontrolled building development.

Mallorca is a good choice for living. Access is usually by air, but there are also excellent ferry services from

Barcelona, Valencia, or Denia. The west coast, from Andratx to Pollenca and the Gallic influence of Soller, is particularly attractive. Palma, the capital, is a clean, bustling city. So there are two sides to Mallorca. The packaged Mallorca concentrated around the Bay of Palma and a far more refined Mallorca, found along the north west coast, in and around old towns like Soller, Valdemossa and Deia.

The northernmost and greenest of the islands is Menorca. It has a cool winter climate and can be prey to powerful north winds. Two attractive old towns lie at either end, Mahon and Ciutadella. Tourism came later here than on the other two islands, and around the coast there are still many beautiful untouched coves and beaches.

Further south than the other islands lies Ibiza. Forget the profusion of spring flowers in February and March. The 24-hour club scene is what brings people here each year.

Canary Islands
Poised on the edge of the tropics west of Morocco, the Canaries enjoy plentiful sunshine, pleasantly cooled by the trade winds. The Canaries have extraordinary volcanic landscapes unlike any other part of Spain and contain no less than four national parks. There are seven islands. Tenerife, Gran Canaria, and Lanzarote are the largest. Housing can be found on all the islands. So too can timeshares, but now restricted by sales regulations.

The landscape of Tenerife is amazing. The scenery ranges from lava desert to forest, from sand dunes to volcanic mountains. It has beaches, banana fields, and at the centre of the island is the highest mountain in Spain, the snow capped volcanic Mount Teide, forming a wilderness of weathered, mineral-tinted rocks. A single road passes through the area, passing a hotel, a cable car station and a visitor's centre.

Artificial grey sand fronts beach resorts on the south west coast clustered around the resort of Playa de las Americas. Los Cristianios, an old fishing port, lies close by and has developed into a pleasant town along the foothills of a barren landscape. Perhaps a better location is on the north coast near the older resort of Puerto de Ia Cruz. It is wetter, greener and away from the maddening crowds.

The capital of Gran Canaria, yet another fine city, is called Las Palmas. Playa del Ingles is a holiday area of high-rise hotel and apartment blocks best avoided. Puerto Rico and Puerto del Morgan on the other hand are attractive, unique, pretty places, quite the opposite to the brash concrete holiday resorts.

Lanzorote is sparsely populated with more goats than people. There is no water. No industry apart from tourism. Solitude, sun worshipping and water sports in a place where time has no meaning.

CASE STUDY – A SPECIAL PLACE

Visitors heading inland from the brash coastal strip of the Costa Blanca are dismayed to find that little English is understood and none spoken except by the ten resident foreigners in the small community of Castell de Castells.

Why should the other 500 Spanish inhabitants even consider another language, as its knowledge is not a prerequisite of a successful rural life?

It is a special place because it has so much history. It is not overrun, as this is impossible in its narrow streets that are virtually impenetrable to modern vehicles and its hills that are exhausting to those on two feet only.

In spring Castells is seen at its best. Wild orchids, rosemary, fennel, thyme and sage grow in abundance. The microclimate achieved from its setting in an amphitheatre of high mountains ensures a change of colour at sunset as the veil of heat lifts from the town. The parched hills of the surrounding sierra turn from brown to green and the distant ridge of mountains to dark blue.

Castells is an hour and a half from Alicante and Valencia but viewed from any perspective it is light years away. The surrounding mountains hold castles agonisingly close to their precipitous tops, looking down, watching over a landscape of high sierras. The Moors have been here too, as many a remaining relic is now testimony to the old Arabic masters.

The main church sits in the city square, which has a bar and a shop. There are a few other places to spend Euros – more shops, a pension, a hotel and a weekly market – but they are for the needs of everyday living as there are no tourists, and no disco bars or wild parties take place here.

At dusk the old village falls strangely silent apart from the old church clock ringing the time. Doors studded with brass buttons silently close. The reflected light of the occasional television screen now flickers in the interiors of houses deliberately kept dark from the invading sunlight during a hot day.

It is a village being regenerated. It has passed through a phase of the young leaving for work on the Costas, for the homing instinct among the young locals remains strong. Family ties remain. As the old die, laid to rest in the small hillside cemetery surrounded by wild flowers, their houses are highly prized for renovation and not easy to come by. The result is that empty ruins are as rare as eagles looking for prey on the hillsides. Houses in the cobbled, narrow back streets give sun and shade in the searing heat as their occupants sit outside and talk, for this is a friendly place where politeness, courtliness and happiness are in order.

The views from houses to the mountains are spectacular and while most foreign homebuyers concentrate on the town and its surroundings, new invaders are searching in some of the far flung villages of Famorca, Facheca, and Tollos: three pretty, high, remote places all within a few minutes drive underneath the high tops of the Sierra de la Serrella which is only shared by rabbits, hares, partridges and quails.

The Spanish residents are sons and daughters of the land, seeking a living from the olive and almond trees while their brothers and sisters down the valley tend to the orange and lemon groves. The quaint green tractors with handlebar steering are quieted for several days as an annual fiesta to celebrate the harvest takes place each December.

What about the ten foreign family residents? They are not your average people, not even your average ex-pats. Villages like Castells will always attract more lucid, outgoing people, at ease with themselves, free from the distractions of modern life and most certainly characters.

COSMOPOLITAN CITIES

Life in a Spanish city normally means living in a large apartment with noisy neighbours. There is nothing wrong with this, as one gets accustomed to the situation. Living in a city brings closeness to facilities such as airports, public transport, shopping, restaurants, nightlife, parks and entertainment. Being near to these facilities means it costs more, but there is always demand for tenants, which is encouraging for the property investor.

Alicante

It is a city with a long history and has for centuries been one of Spain's most important ports. It is the regional capital of the Costa Blanca and its main service centre. The city boasts several important monuments, including Santa Barbara Castle and the nationally famous, palm tree-lined marble promenade known as the *Explanada*. The old quarter, known as Santa Cruz, is one of the city's most attractive areas, with its narrow, pedestrian streets.

Alicante is an important business centre and offers a wide range of hotel accommodation. There are several attractive beaches within the city boundaries.

Excellent shopping facilities exist, with a range of department stores, shopping centres and international boutiques. The residential area is popular because of its proximity to the city's amenities. The city also boasts a new shopping area where many of the chain stores are now located.

Along with the rest of the Costa Blanca, Alicante has a mild, pleasant climate for much of the year, although it can be very hot in the summer.

Barcelona

If you are looking for premier city living then this unquestionably is the place. One of the Mediterranean's busiest ports, it is much more than the capital of Catalonia. Culturally, commercially and in sport it not only rivals Madrid, but also rightfully considers itself on a par with the greatest European cities. The success of the Olympic Games confirmed this to the world. It is always open to outside influences because of its location on the coast, not far from the French border.

Las Ramblas is the most famous street in Spain. It is busy round the clock, especially in the evenings and at weekends. News-stands, caged birds, flower stalls, tarot readers, musicians and mime artists throng the wide, tree-shaded, central walkway.

Camp Nou is one of Europe's largest football stadiums, home to the city's famous football club with its fanatical, critical supporters. Its magnificent sweeping structure befits one of the world's richest clubs. Barcelona FC more than anything else is a symbol of Catalan nationalism pitted against the central government of Madrid. To fail to win the league is one thing, to come behind Real Madrid is a complete disaster.

Barcelona is a city with impeccable style and vitality, demonstrated by the very best of Catalan, Spanish and International fashion design and complemented by a stunning live arts scene as it regularly plays host to some of the world's best musicians.

Situated in Catalonia it presents a picture of a proud nation within a nation, with its own language, Catalan, which has all but replaced Spanish in place names and on road signs throughout the region.

Granada

Granada is a small city in Andalucia, sitting behind the high mountains of the Sierra Nevada. It lies in a fertile plain surrounded by almost permanently snow-covered mountains and is one of Spain's major tourist cities. Granada marks the final stand of Moorish rule in Spain, and also its most glorious manifestation. The Moors were retreating south when Granada was first fortified in the 13th century, and the Alhambra Palace now assures Granada worldwide fame. It is considered to be the finest example of Moorish architecture in the world. The layout of the grand rooms, gardens and water features can be marvelled at for hours. Built mainly in the 14th century, the Alhambra's patios, pavilions and banqueting hall served the Moorish rulers until their final expulsion from Spain in 1492, the same year that Columbus discovered the Americas.

It is also an important university city and a cosmopolitan place to live. Granada's total population is around 230,000, with few foreign residents. It has a typical continental climate, with cold, dry winters and hot summers. The proximity of the snow-covered Sierra Nevada means that night temperatures are often below freezing in winter and cool even at the height of summer.

Malaga

Malaga is Spain's fifth largest city. It is the capital of the Costa del Sol and a major Mediterranean port. It is one of the most cosmopolitan cities in Spain and for centuries has been a popular destination for foreigners, as the names of many of the city's districts and streets testify. During the 19th century, Malaga was a thriving winter resort for wealthy Europeans.

Malaga has been largely untouched by mass tourism and remains a genuine Andalucian city. The city's Moorish history, as with many other Andalucian capitals, can clearly be seen in the Alcazaba fortress and the Gibralfaro castle, now home to a luxury hotel. It has the best amenities and facilities on the Costa del Sol. The city has a vibrant cultural scene, with concerts and other events all year round. It also has excellent shopping facilities. Although Malaga is busy, it does not become crowded. It is typically Spanish, has severe traffic congestion, and is several degrees hotter than the rest of the Costa del Sol in summer, particularly when an offshore wind blows.

Modern Malaga is situated on the west side of the Guadalmedina River around the large department stores and the shopping centre, which encompasses many of the city's amenities, including the bus and railway stations. The old town centre, which is full of narrow streets around the cathedral, is being restored.

Madrid

Situated in the centre of the country the capital Madrid is a city of over three million people and a crossroads for rail, road and air travel befitting a modern capital. Its altitude of 660 metres gives rise to a temperature profile of cold winters and hot summers, making spring and autumn the best times to visit. Those who can escape from Madrid during August make for the cooler north or south to the Mediterranean.

Despite the climate the capital city has developed its own unique personality. It boasts the *Parque del Retiro,* a world-famous area of leafy paths and avenues, a royal palace and grand public squares. Its museums are filled with Spain's historic treasures. The Museo del Prado contains the world's greatest assembly of Spanish painting, particularly the works of Valazquez and Goya. It also houses impressive foreign collections.

Madrid is a city that offers the best in shopping facilities. The latest designer clothes are sold in elegant up-market stores. There are food markets throughout the city. The centuries-old *Rastro*, open every Sunday, is one of the world's greatest flea markets.

There is a good choice of music. Classical, jazz and rock compete with Madrid's own comic style opera known as *zarzuela*. Saturday night starts in the cafes then moves to the *tapas* bars, restaurants or clubs, revelling throughout the night and adding to the city's clamouring traffic noise.

Sevilla

El Arenal, a district of Sevilla, was once home to an ammunition factory and artillery headquarters but now the atmosphere is set by the city's majestic bullring called the Plaza de Toros de la Maestranza. During the bull-fighting season the bars and restaurants are packed, but for the rest of the year the wide Quadalquivir River is enjoyed by many on boat trips. The *barrio* of Santa Cruz is Sevilla's other district. It was the old Jewish quarter; a warren of white alleyways and flower decked patios, now representing Sevilla at its most romantic and compact. The maze of narrow streets hides *tapas* bars, plazas, and up-market residences. Ornamental orange trees line the streets, the fruit with a bittersweet taste only suitable for making marmalade. It was, however, Expo 92 that focused world attention on Sevilla where over one hundred countries were represented in the many pavilions which displayed scientific, technological and cultural exhibits.

Although hot, Sevilla has excellent shopping facilities with some European chain stores represented in modern streets. Premier living is available in this city where all the stereotypes of Andalucia meet in its capital. By travelling only a few kilometres from the city walls the rural delights of the countryside open up and detached white-walled properties set on hillsides are to be seen.

Valencia

This attractive, historic city has the advantage of being a few miles inland from the sea. Here it is possible to enjoy beaches as the Spanish enjoy them, because they have never been developed for mass tourism. Valencia is very much a Mediterranean city, famous as the birthplace of the rice dish paella, and is also renowned for its oranges. The annual festival Las Fallas draws people from all over world where monster-sized effigies, which have taken a year to build, are burnt in a glorious night of pyrotechnics.

With its large car manufacturing plants Valencia is an industrialised city but in contrast the largest science museum in Europe opened in 2000 and the Oceanographic two years later. These attractions are a cornerstone of its new development with the 225 million Euro science museum an imposing new landmark on the edge of the city centre resembling a huge white animal skeleton with glass walls and a spiny structure of pointed arches. The science museum takes an interactive approach and includes three floors of permanent exhibits concentrating on telecommunications, a window to the world of science, a virtual fishbowl, metals and minerals and art forms.

The Oceanographic is the largest attraction of its kind in Europe, devoted to all aspects of the sea and marine life. It is set to become a major attraction in drawing visitors to the city.

Valencia has a strong Spanish flavour. A modern promenade lined with restaurants runs along the beach for several miles, and the area around Las Arenas is very fashionable.

OTHER INTERESTING PLACES

There is more to Spain than coastal resorts and large cities. Other places exist, some old and tired, less populated, or more rural, sometimes wet and green, perhaps known only to Spaniards and on occasion waiting for development to arrive.

The Costa del Azahar

This is the name given to the coast of Valencia and it means Orange Blossom Coast, which is highly appropriate since orange groves cover the large fertile plain. To the south lies Albufera, a huge area of freshwater wetlands celebrated for its bird life. The rice used in paella and other local dishes is grown here.

This is a playground for Spaniards. Spanish families from Valencia or Madrid, rather than foreigners, buy property here. Gandia, Cullera and Peniscola are all historic old towns, popular as Spanish family resorts, busy in summer, but empty the rest of the year.

Costa Brava

In the 1960s the rugged Costa Brava (Wild Coast) became one of Europe's first mass package holiday destinations. Communications are good, the motorway from France enters Eastern Spain continuing through the region on its long way south to Gibraltar. The area is also well served by train and bus services.

The small towns along the coast north of Barcelona are becoming part of a commuter belt to the city. The coastal strip is very narrow because a steep mountain ridge rises up behind it, and most of the towns have a lower, beach half and an upper part at the top of the hill.

It is perhaps better to miss the mass tourist resorts of Loret del Mar, Tossa del Mar, La Platja d'Oro, and Salou. But on the coast some smaller towns are well worth a visit as is the inland town of Girona set on the River Onyar.

Costa Calida

The southern end of the Costa Blanca, administered by Murcia, is now called the Costa Calida or Hot Coast and claims the well known attractions of Mar Menor, a shallow almost land-locked part of the Mediterranean. Nearby is La Manga, a playground for the rich, where pampered sporting activities and expensive homes in exclusive surroundings are the order of the day. Three golf courses and many other world class facilities have made La Manga famous by providing winter training facilities for top-class football teams.

The main centre is Cartagena, the Mediterranean home of the Spanish Navy, a deep land-locked harbour now used as a stopping place for luxury cruise liners. It is unspoilt by tourism, has many unusual buildings associated with a long naval tradition and interesting Roman remains. Mazarron and its resort of Puerto de Mazarron has fine beaches, a marina and cheap housing for those who wish to soak up the sun and play golf but prefer not to get to grips with Spanish culture.

It may be bleak, barren and dusty. It is certainly hot, but it is the last strip of Mediterranean coast to be developed ... and it will be developed (see property hot spot later in this chapter).

Costa Dorada

The Catalan coast south of Barcelona is known as the Costa Dorada. It is Barcelona's favourite weekend beach. Sitges is a family resort but has remained trendy with a thriving artists' colony. Salou is the tourist hub of the area but has nothing to really commend it.

Costa de la Luz

The Coast of Light is situated to the west of Gibraltar facing the Atlantic. Spain's southernmost tip is an unspoilt, windswept stretch of coast characterised by strong pure light – hence it's name. Other than Cadiz which is almost entirely surrounded by water; Jerez the capital of sherry production and the Donana National Park, an area of wetlands, sand dunes and marshland, the region has little to commend it.

Central Spain

The vast central plateau of Spain is covered in dry dusty plains and large rolling fields. Given the attractions of the Costas and the Islands it is not an area where many northern Europeans settle. It is a place of work. Long straight roads, vast fields devoted to wheat, sunflowers and the grape dominate the region. It is remote, of stunning beauty, suitable for those engaged in agriculture or for those who want to get off the beaten track and go back to nature.

Regions such as Castilla Leon and Castilla La Mancha, Aragon and Extremadura are remote with towns stuck in a time warp. Some villages are on the tops of hills, some in barren rift valleys, some barely inhabited and some seemingly inhabited only by green tractors. This is not rural Spain. It is certainly not Green Spain. It is old Spain.

It is easy to find remote, cheap houses for sale, all requiring considerable work for those who wish to avoid all human contact and live life in the crawler lane, dreaming of the adventures of Don Quixote (for he is caricatured in metal figures everywhere). But letting potential – absolutely nil.

Gibraltar

Gibraltar is not in Spain but should be mentioned as it sits to the south of the country. It is part of the United Kingdom but not part of the EU. Economically it stands alone. A strange piece of land, its future as a strategic entrance to the Mediterranean seems less important as time goes by. For a small community, isolated from the rest of Spain by artificial political barriers, the future is uncertain. The economy of the Rock depends on a naval dockyard, tourism, tax-free shopping and financial services.

Green Spain

Increasing numbers of people are discovering the deep green landscapes, the solitude of the mountains and the quiet sandy beaches of northern Spain. The Atlantic coast from the Portuguese border to the Pyrenees is often scenic but no more so than the cliffs of Galicia and the Picos mountains. Inland the mild but wet climate has created lush green meadows and broad-leaved forests.

To the west in Asturias and Cantabria, the most obvious attraction is the group of mountains called the Picos de Europa that straddles the two communities. To the east lie the Pyrenees, joining Spain to France by a vast fortress of rock and snow. These mountains, set in two national parks, offer excellent rock climbing and good hiking but in winter, when covered in snow, are extremely dangerous.

Some people say this area is like Scotland, Ireland, Wales and England rolled into one. Mild, wet and definitely green. Just like being at home but with a different culture. The Swiss too lay claim to the country, saying the Picos and Pyrenees are similar to their Alps.

A PROPERTY HOT SPOT

Not all properties appreciate in price at the same rate. Some go up much faster than others. Buy in a fast appreciating area for a bigger, quicker profit. Some areas such as the Costa Blanca are lower in price and will move up faster. But it would be a mistake to think that hot spot areas are only regional by nature. Within any given town there may be some *barrios* that shoot up in price, while others simply stagnate.

Neglected areas may be ripe for a turnaround. Parts of some blighted cities are the target of renovation funds from local government supported by EU grant aid. Equally old Spanish villages, abandoned only a few years ago, can suddenly look attractive investments. The key is to find such an area in a turnaround phase, and then buy into it. Within a few years, residential property values should increase.

The real question becomes, how do you identify the next hot spot area? There are at least three different indicators that suggest where and when an area is about to take off:

- A high volume of resales.
- Lots of new development.
- Rapidly increasing prices.

While local people can recommend local hot spots, or mountain villages that can suddenly look like an attractive pacesetting development, is there an area of Spain where residential property values should rapidly increase within the next 10 to 20 years? One that meets the definition of a good long-term investment? The answer is yes. It is called the Costa Calida, in the Region de Murcia and touched on briefly earlier in this chapter.

To date Murcia is a forgotten area on the Spanish Mediterranean coast. Looking at Murcia's own Costa Calida, with the possible exception of La Manga no well-known names can be found. How long will this last? As to the north, the Costa Blanca has the unstoppable development of cheap holiday homes in Torrevieja and further south, the Costa del Sol beckons, now well worn, almost deserving of its poor reputation.

The most popular resorts of Murcia's 'Hot Coast' are around the Mar Menor. The few small beaches are dwarfed by cliffs and headlands. The resorts of the southern part of the coast are relatively quiet for Spain. There are several fine beaches at Puerto de Mazarron. The growing resort of Aguilas marks the southern limit of the border with Andalucia.

The natural harbour of Cartagena was constucted in 223 BC by the Carthaginians who called it Quart Hadas (New City). After conquering the city the Romans renamed it Carthago Nova (New Carthage). Although the city declined in importance in the Middle Ages, its prestige increased in the 18th century when it became a major naval base. It is possible to get an overview of the city from the park which surrounds the ruins of Cartagena's castle, the Castilio de la Concepcion.

The port was Hannibal's Iberian stronghold and the landing place for his expeditionary elephants, and he was followed by the Romans and the Moors, whose legacy can be seen in the winding narrow streets. Excavations in the city include a Roman street and the Muralla Bizantina (Byzantine Wall) built between 589 and 590.

The elongated high-rise holiday resort of La Manga, built on a long, thin sandy strip, separates the Mediterranean from the Mar Menor, literally 'the smaller sea', but really a large coastal lagoon of 170 square kilometres of warm seawater. It has a unique marine environment where seahorses flourish, cut off from their natural predators by the formation of the spit. The sheltered Mar Menor can be five degrees warmer than the Mediterranean. In the early 20th century its high mineral concentrations first drew tourists for rest cure. They stayed at the older resort of Los Alcazares, which still has wooden jetties protruding from the beach.

A mile or so away lies the La Manga Club, founded by an American called Peters as a Florida-style resort. Residents on its 1,400 well-tended acres, of whom at least 60% are British, have three golf courses, tennis courts, football pitches, swimming pools, restaurants, bars and a five star hotel at their disposal.

There are plans to raise the region's profile and the Murcia government is going about it in a sound logical way. New airports and two new projects for the marinas at Aguilas and at Mazarron are planned. Seven seafront golf courses are proposed and 25,000 more hotel beds. Between the coast and the capital Murcia, near the small country town of Fuente Alamo, a grand vision is being realised. On a 600 hectare expanse of gently sloping brown earth, formerly given over to market gardening, two 18-hole golf courses and more than 2,800 homes are planned. It is a tranquil setting, surrounded by largely empty motorways with the Hacienda del Alamo aiming to rival the La Manga Club in popularity.

If you want a hot coast, and a property hot spot too, look to the Costa Calida for a long-term investment.

SUMMARY

- The main areas of attraction for sun, sea and sand will always be the principal Costas – Costa del Sol and the Costa Blanca, and the main islands – the Balearic and Canaries.

- Living in a city means being close to amenities and to potential tenants. The principal cities are of course Madrid and Barcelona, but Alicante, Granada, Malaga, Sevilla and Valencia all have good facilities.

- There are other Costas, green northern Spain, the vast central plateau and even Gibraltar to consider. All have advantages and opportunities for buying and letting.

- A property hot spot area – try the Costa Calida.

6

What to Buy

CONSIDERING DIFFERENT HOUSE TYPES

Urbanisations

Spain is a land of urbanisations, which is a continental name for housing estates. They may line the beach, be in the country, attached to towns, villages or resorts, they may be on flat land, on hills or around sporting facilities such as golf courses. They can be high-density estates of identical white properties, or small individual developments of big detached houses spread over a hillside. Or, more likely, they will be various combinations in-between.

A property on an urbanisation is easy to buy and maintain, having all the necessary facilities, ready-made social contacts and greater security than owning a detached home in a more remote location. The disadvantages can be the inflexible and restrictive community rules, difficult neighbours, a lack of privacy and a lack of control over the future of the development.

Life on an urbanisation can, however, be popular whatever the type of house. Sitting by the swimming pool meeting new continental friends, passing the time of day with a glass of wine in hand is an agreeable way of life. Little Spanish is spoken. Sharing experiences bonds the community together. Informal groupings take place. Golfing partners come together. Coffee mornings just happen. Family problems are shared. The siesta is forgotten as people assemble in the local bar to escape the searing heat of the afternoon sun. Life is easy. However it is very important for mind and body to stay active or a slow soporific mental decline will occur.

Some urbanisations are closed communities where people meet up at night and know each other's business. Others are less intrusive. Some are entirely of one nationality while others are more mixed. In some most of the residents are elderly. Some urbanisations are a group of holiday homes scarcely having any permanent residents, and becoming virtual ghost towns in winter.

Is a property on an urbanisation a good rental proposition? The answer is yes, particularly with foreigners holidaying in Spain who can meet up with people of their own nationality for sporting and social occasions.

Detached villas
These properties offer privacy at the expense of security. They can be expensive. Built to an individual design they

are sometimes perched precariously on cutaway hillsides, so much so that insurance companies can charge a premium. Windswept plots make dust a perpetual irritant. Even with some disadvantages a detached property is desirable, particularly one that overlooks the sea or the mountains or even a lush green golf course. They are more expensive than a house of similar size and comfort on an urbanisation, but the advantages are privacy and no community of owners to deal with. With a swimming pool they are prized letting properties.

Villa properties are attractive for up-market tenants soaking up the summer sun while on their annual holiday. They tend to be the houses of owners seeking to defray some of their annual expenses by letting out the property. A buy-to-let investor should think carefully before acquiring such an expensive property, let out only for a short season, when the alternative could be four cheaper apartments let out for longer periods.

Apartments

Choosing to live in an apartment offers easy living in secure surroundings. In order to sell apartments quickly they are always built to a high standard, with outside balconies included. Some basic economy flats exist in large cities where low cost living is a priority. Living in an apartment will probably mean Spanish neighbours, as urban Spaniards are traditionally apartment dwellers, with more floor space than some UK semi-detached or detached houses. Nice people they may well be, but they tend to be noisy and have a different 'body clock' to other nationalities. Normal behaviour is to rise late, have lunch at 2.00 p.m., an evening meal at 9.00 p.m. and go to bed at midnight or after. Family discussion is often loud, very loud, Spanish voices having the unique ability to penetrate all bricks and mortar.

Holiday apartments are meat and drink to a buy-to-let investor. They are small, flexible housing units. A large number of holiday apartments have been built along the coast. Many are designed for pretty undemanding tenants residing about two weeks at a time. They offer limited comfort for a long-term stay. It is often these apartments that are used for basic holiday rentals. An equally large number of apartments are available in cities, towns and villages but designed and furnished for longer stay tenants.

Traditional homes
Older Spanish properties exist in small towns and villages that often have a number of cool, shady rooms. Houses on a slope often have several floors, balconies and internal courtyards invisible from the street and of great character. In most cases they have been modernised or rebuilt. They are called reformed houses. A reformed town house is in many respects an ideal property since it gives easy access to the town with the benefits of living in new modern surroundings. They offer good Buy to Let opportunities for Spanish tenants but foreign tenants find it difficult to integrate into the local community.

Fincas
A _finca_ is normally a sizable property, usually set on a substantial amount of land in the countryside. It is a

pleasant place to 'get away from it all' but can be considered too large or too remote for renting. For a resident, it is where dreams are made. It can be a labour of love, with considerable skill, determination and money required in order to succeed in rebuilding an old crumbling building into a individual, personalised property of pride and charm. Renovating a property, or indeed maintaining it, demands very good DIY skills. Living in one needs patience, a degree of tolerance and some enthusiasm to deal with everyday problems.

A PERSONALITY *FINCA*

What makes the difference between a real old *finca* and a modern reformed house? Not just its age but also the greenery that slowly and magically grows around a human habitation. The mature trees and the familiar sounds that make an ancient house an individual home. Not to mention the birds that live in the eaves, bats in the attic and kestrels that hover over the field at the back.

The personality of a house can be no greater than in an old *finca* where generations of families have left their imprint on the building and its surroundings, so that every window, fireplace, corridor and cupboard reflect history. A *finca* surrounded by well tended land gets better as it grows older.

Modern *finca* restorations tend to replicate the old with large beams and fancy hallways. Personality is forced and imposed through its layout by the building work and the materials used. A fine balance has to be achieved between the old and the new. The windows and outside doors usually make a statement in dark oak giving an impression of instant ageing. There is just enough reclaimed timber and floor bricks to take the edge off the newness of the building, without it looking antique. Then there are the fireplaces, a focus of warmth in every sense and a home to the traditional Spanish metal wood-burning stove or enhanced into a big open fireplace.

How can a new house compete with all this? But character is not the only factor to be considered in recreating the old as it invariably costs more than the new and, while it may be a home, is it a rental proposition?

A VISION FOR THE FUTURE

Before buying, a buy-to-let investor should check that the local town council has a vision for its future ... and yours. Why? To make sure that it is providing up-to-date facilities for its citizens and looking after the basic needs of roads, lighting and cleaning. Some urban councils seem to take a view that their main preoccupation in life is to constantly beautify the *Ermita* (a religious building set atop a hill and lined with slender conifers). Checking the vision is not too difficult. Here are the excellent published objectives for one major city:

> Our yearly challenge is to ensure that visitors to our city take home unforgettable memories. It is both an exciting and compelling mission for everyone involved in promoting the city, and one that gets easier every year as we continue to improve and innovate.

> Our city development has been controlled since the early 1950s when a plan was approved which created a new model maintaining a balance with the surrounding environment. New projects reflect this approach. Under

the programme the town council is studying ways to protect and regenerate the bird and marine life of natural habitats in the area, while also setting aside access for recreational purposes. Other new initiatives include special facilities that have been installed to enable physically challenged visitors to enjoy the city's beaches.

The collaboration between city hall, local businesses and the people of the city makes for a great team. Working together we will make sure our unique destination merits a vote of confidence, as much for the quality of service it provides as for the satisfaction and unforgettable memories it generates.

There's always a warm welcome awaiting people here.

Look for the town plan called the *Plan General de Ordenacion Urbana*. Drawing it up involves both local and regional governments. It involves political, social and legal change. A town plan is not a static document. It can involve strategic planning and detailed consideration of individual planning applications. In areas of outstanding beauty, retaining the natural charm is often a key issue.

Smaller Town Halls publish monthly a *Bulletin de Informacion Municipal*. It is usually a brightly coloured document giving details of public works, announcements, social activities, local holidays and fiestas.

Transparency in the political life of Spain is never an issue.

BUYING A SPANISH HOME

What do we really want when buying a Spanish home? Is it a property close to the sea with easy access to the countryside, a town and an airport? Is it to be new, white, set in a large plot of land? Do restaurants, pubs, hospitals, doctors and dentists have to be close by? Are neighbours only to be British, Irish and the rather pleasant Dutch?

No, not really! What we do is to set a number of priorities, which are usually the price, the number of bedrooms, the type of house and the location. Then we look for Position and Character.

Position is location. Overlooking orange and lemon groves! Close to a pine-filled ravine! At the edge of purple hills! Next to a marina! More simply it can be exotic gardens or a house that has obviously been well-loved and cared for. Position is that little bit extra making a property highly desirable – and probably that little bit more expensive. It is no good buying a large detached property surrounded by cheap flats. It will just lose value. A property at the end of a street, facing a commercial centre will suffer the same fate. A property in the middle of a row of similar houses has nothing to commend it. Future resale values are dependent on the general ambience of the area.

Character is a personal thing: something that makes a property just that little bit different. Is it an individual detached property that has a number of unique features? How about porches, terraces for sitting in the sun and enjoying a glass of wine? Or a swimming pool perhaps? Large, white, airy rooms with walls covered in colourful pictures? Whatever it is, in the eye of the beholder, it is that something special that makes a house a desirable home to live in.

BUYING A SPANISH RENTAL PROPERTY

What do we really want when purchasing a buy-to-let property? Simple answer – one that is easy to let, easy to run and has no problems!

To get good tenants a property must be in a good area. If the property does not appeal, who is going to rent it? The better the area, the easier it is to rent. Homes in good areas are always in demand, while those in run down areas languish. On the other hand, do not buy in the very best areas. They are often over-priced, such as Marbella, and it is difficult to buy a property that will rent for enough to cover the monthly costs.

It is better to buy rental property in areas where most of the residences are owner-occupied. The neighbours may not love this idea, but tenants will. If an area is mostly tenant-occupied, such as a student area, there will also be a lot of competition.

Smaller properties are generally more desirable to rent. They are often located in better areas and they attract a better class of tenants. The more people who occupy a property, then the more wear and tear. Does that mean that a one bedroom house makes a good rental? It can be for a student or businessman in a city. Two and three bedroom properties make good rentals. Four and five bedroom properties most certainly do not, unless they are premium luxury villas overlooking the sea.

Like a big garden? Then buy a house with a big garden to live in. But, as an investor, avoid them like the plague. A big garden requires a lot of maintenance. If it has lots of shrubs and landscaping, a gardener is required. Do not count on a tenant to water the garden. On the other hand, properties with swimming pools make an attractive proposition to those tenants who wish to take a relaxing holiday in the sun. Cooling the body parts in the villa pool is often seen as an essential requirement for letting.

Do not purchase a picturesque tumbledown farmhouse only to discover that renovation is way beyond personal skills and means. Either that, or get hopelessly bogged down in bureaucracy trying to get planning permission and satisfying all the requirements of building regulations. It is all too easy to become entangled in the red tape if not conversant with Spanish laws, or not speaking the language fluently.

Always try to buy a newer property, as it will save a fortune on maintenance costs. Consider what may occur. Plumbing failure from leaking pipes. Electrical failure from light switches and plugs that suddenly burn out. Worn out appliances. A new house, preferably one less than ten years old will largely avoid such problems.

Buying far from home may cause problems. A small investor is directly involved in the management of the property. A small investor is the person who has to take the decisions. Living in Manchester with a second property in Spain can result in small tasks mushrooming into big problems. There is the question of who looks after the place in the owner's absence. Some owners retain a friendly local to keep an eye on the property, to clean it or to hand over the keys to tenants.

IT'S A BALANCE

Underlining the previous comments – do not fall in love with an investment house. When you buy a Spanish home to live in you're allowed to fall in love with the house. When you buy to invest, you're not. A buy-to-let for fun and profit is a balance between the two. The tiled floors, the attractive archway and the white walls have a place in the decision-making process but questions that also need to be asked have to do with price, tenants and the ease of renting.

SUMMARY

◆ The property type can be a detached villa, a high-rise apartment, a traditional town house or a rural *finca*. All have pros and cons for buying and letting.

◆ A property can be on a popular urbanisation, in the remote countryside, on flat land or on a hillside, or even in a town or city. All have pros and cons for buying and letting.

◆ Before buying ensure the local Town Hall has a vision for its future – and yours.

◆ There are guidelines for buying a Spanish home and there are different guidelines for buying a rental property. A buy-to-let is a balance between the two.

$$\boxed{7}$$

Buying Sensibly

THE AGENT CAN BE A FRIEND

By virtue of their daily contacts, estate agents know who are buying and selling. The top agents keep files of buyers, sellers and specialised properties. It is not unusual for a good agent, when he learns of a new listing, to sell it within 24 hours to a buyer he knows will buy that type of property. An agent, given time and a detailed specification, will always find a property for a determined buyer. He may have to be chased occasionally but that is part of the process of being determined.

Spanish estate agents have a curious name – *inmobiliaria*, a word almost suggesting that 'a person does not move'. Yet in Spain these people are very common – small local estate agents who know their patch well, concentrating mainly on resale properties. They need not be Spanish and indeed many are German, Scandinavian or British.

It is a good idea to deal with a registered estate agent. In Spain they belong to the *Agente de Propiedad Inmobiliaria*, have a certificate of registration and an identification number. They can be sued if anything goes wrong. Dealing with such a registered business gives the purchaser more security and confidence.

There are always stories in Spain of people losing their life savings because they have dealt with an unscrupulous estate agent. They may have bought a house only to discover the person selling it did not own it in the first place. The only real way to avoid this is to deal with a registered agent whose number should be on a sign outside the office, on a window display or on the exterior of the building.

The quality of estate agents has vastly improved in the last few years. Selling houses attracts some of the finest people. But it also attracts some of the more unscrupulous characters too, probably because it is possible to earn a handsome income without working too hard. Due to its financial structure the estate agency business opens doors to all types of people some of which are not completely honest. If horror stories are heard about buying Spanish properties they usually start here with the agent.

But if you get suspicious and nervous when dealing with an agent you should relax. First of all, most agents aren't thieves and swindlers. If anything, they're more honest than the average person because they have their licences and their business reputations to protect.

Agents dealing in Spanish property do take a high commission. The lowest start at around 3% but the average is 10%. When selling a country house (*finca*) it can be 25%. How do they justify such exhorbitant charges? Their answer is ambiguous, making reference to high advertising costs, commissions due in two countries and complex transactions involving different nationalities. In truth it is simply a seller's market with demand outstripping supply, causing many people to enter the lucrative business of house selling.

The commission rate for selling a new house on behalf of a builder is usually fixed at around 10%. If a number of agents are selling the same property they may compete with each other, discounting their commission.

A different commission structure operates for the sale of a second-hand property, commonly termed a resale property. In some cases the agent operates on a fixed commission, but the following arrangement is more customary:

- The agent asks the seller the price he wishes for the property.

- He advertises and negotiates the sale of the property at another, higher price.

- The difference between the two prices is the agent's commission.

Property buyers in many European countries are carefully protected during a major financial transaction. They are even protected from their own mistakes by the right to withdraw from an agreement for up to several weeks after signing the appropriate contract. They should be a little bit more wary in Spain where the *Notario*, a representative of the Spanish government, only carries out the regulation of conveyancing at the final stage.

CASE STUDY – ON THE SLOPES

Jenny and Paul came together in their middle years. The result was two properties. To live in the best one, an apartment overlooking the sea, and rent out the other was the obvious thing to do. After a few years a rethink took place. 'Lets sell the tenanted apartment,' said Paul, which was purely for financial gain, 'and buy another one in Granada for fun and profit'. To be precise at *Solynieve* (sun and snow).

Hundreds of skiers travel from all parts of Spain to the Sierra Nevada each year to enjoy the southernmost ski centre in mainland Europe and also one of the highest, giving a long season with good sunshine, lasting until May. Just outside Granada the resort is well developed with parking for thousands of cars and buses, 19 ski lifts capable of carrying 30,000 people per hour, 54 kilometres of marked slopes (3.5 kilometres floodlit for night time skiing at weekends) and 17 hotels.

They bought a sturdily built apartment made mainly from wood, which they enjoy for their frequent skiing trips. In the summer they go hiking in the mountains and sightseeing in the ancient Moorish city of Granada. Tenants, mainly skiers, are found by a rental agency at a cost of 22.5% of rental income. The agency looks after cleaning and maintenance too!

And the sequel – so successful has the venture been – they have now bought another apartment in the same block.

TAKING LEGAL ADVICE

There are many excellent local lawyers *(abogados)* in Spain who are fluent in English. A lawyer will ensure that Spanish legal requirements are met, the property is bought free of encumbrances, charges, loans or debt and up-to-date payments to local services and community charges (if applicable) have been made.

Prior to viewing a Spanish property you should make sure that you have at your disposal sufficient funds to cover a deposit. The deposit may be paid with a credit card or cash, but usually cash. A cheque drawn on a foreign bank may take up to ten days to clear by a Spanish bank. Once a suitable property has been chosen, the purchase terms and price will need to be verbally agreed with the seller. An offer may be made subject to mortgage approval, completion dates and the method of payment.

Once there is verbal accord between parties, the next step is to formalise the terms in writing by exchange of a private contract of sale. This may take place within two weeks following formal acceptance of the offer or sooner. The lawyer will have completed his searches and investigation of the property and will have arranged with the owner the procedure for cancellation of any outstanding debts. The private Purchase and Sale Contract will reflect all the agreed terms and set out the date for final completion at the *Notary*. It is customary practice at this stage to pay a 10% deposit of the purchase price which normally is non-refundable should the purchaser fail to complete.

A sale is formally completed in Spain when the title deed (*Escritura*) is signed before a *Notary*, the final payment made, and possession given to the buyer. Once signed, the *Notary* will fax a note of the title deed to the local land registry. The lawyer will also pay on the buyer's behalf all the relevant transfer taxes associated with the purchase and will handle the formalities of registration of the title deeds. Final registration of the deed may take up to six months. Similarly, the lawyer will arrange for the transfer of utility services, such as water and electricity, and organise future payments through the client's bank account.

It cannot be emphasised too strongly that anyone planning to buy a property in Spain must take independent legal advice in a language in which they are fluent from a lawyer experienced in Spanish property law. Always deal with professionals and do not assume that in dealing with a fellow countryman the advice is better, cheaper or even unbiased.

Do not sign anything, or pay a deposit, until legal advice has been obtained. Once the advice is given – take it. Do not assume it is someone dotting the i's and crossing the t's. One of the most common phrases heard in Spain is about buyers 'leaving their brains behind at the airport'. It is true! The rush to buy a home, pressurised decision-making or the euphoria of the moment can often make people do incredibly stupid things like literally handing over cash deposits to agents or owners with little or no security.

Full details of Spanish legal procedures can be found in *Buying a Property in Spain* by Harry King, also published by How to Books.

FINDING THE MONEY

Most people who buy a permanent home in Spain do so outright. Most people who have a second property require additional capital. Loans from a bank, or a remortgage of the main residence are popular choices. The relatively free availability of money means that lenders in Britain are quite relaxed about homeowners using the equity in their UK homes to fund the purchase of a second property overseas.

Spanish banks offer mortgages at attractive rates. There are no Spanish Building Societies. Spanish Banks therefore have a captive market for the provision of domestic home finance. The criteria for a mortgage are quite familiar:

- The earnings of one or both purchasers are taken into account.

- Most importantly, the property is valued not at market value, but at a rebuild cost per square metre.

- The maximum mortgage for a non resident is around 60% of the valuation. The maximum for a resident is around 80%.

- A combination of low valuation based on rebuilding cost and not market value, and low mortgage based on that valuation, means the actual mortgage can be as low as 40% of the market price of the property.

A number of lenders, such as Abbey National, Halifax, Norwich & Peterborough Building Society and Royal Bank of Scotland offer mortgages on properties in Spain through their offices in Gibraltar and Spain. The mighty Deutsche Bank and French BNP are also active in this market.

A Euro denominated mortgage is calculated on a different basis compared to rates charged on UK Sterling denominated mortgages. Spanish mortgage rates are commonly quoted as Euribor plus a percentage. So for example a mortgage advisement will state 'Euribor + 1%'. Euribor is the Interbank lending rate used across the entire Euro zone. As such, it is used as a common benchmark for consumer borrowing across a wide range of loans including credit cards and mortgages.

If you earn in Sterling, borrow in Sterling and repay in Sterling. Similarly if you earn in Euros, borrow in Euros and repay in Euros. When currencies move, the asset and income moves in the same direction as the mortgage. A Spanish mortgage means a Euro mortgage, which means you borrow and repay in that currency. For someone living and working in Spain and earning in Euros this makes sense, but if you are a UK resident with your income paid in Sterling, borrowing in Euros and earning in Sterling comprises a currency risk.

When considering the relative merits of each lender's interest rate, currency and mechanism, there is another vital point to consider. Spanish lenders, including British based lenders with offices in Spain and Gibraltar, are less generous than their UK based counterparts when taking into account personal earnings multipliers and property valuation.

PAYING THE MONEY

Buying off-plan

Prospective buyers visiting property exhibitions in the UK are often given the opportunity to buy a property 'off-plan'. This means homes, whole or part urbanisations, that have not yet been built; looking at a plan of the property with the room sizes in square metres, a plan of the development and viewing a show home form the basis of the decision. The contract should state the date of completion and penalties for failure of either party to complete on time. Payments are made in instalments:

  10% on signing the contract
  40% stage payment
  25% stage payment
  25% on completion.

Buying a resale property

The payments are:

  10% on signing the contract
  90% on completion.

Buying a partly built property

The payments are:

  50% on signing the contract (walls, roof, windows and doors completed)
  25% stage payment
  25% on completion.

Buying costs

It is normal to allow 10% of the property value declared in the *escritura* for the additional costs in buying which covers three taxes, two fees and charges from a lawyer. A breakdown of these costs is as follows:

- Transfer tax or IVA (value added tax)   7%
- Stamp duty on a new property only   0.5%
- *Plus Valia* tax   0.5%
- Notary fees   0.5%
- Property Register fees   0.5%
- Charges from the *abogado* (lawyer)   1.0%

SPENDING WISELY

Buy-to-let for fun and profit is an investment decision. Never pay an inflated price for a property. True value is hard to judge in a rising property market. However, checking comparable sales is the greatest assistance in valuation.

Always offer below what the seller is asking. How far below? An offer that is 10% below asking price is not unreasonable. This technique definitely works in a cold market but is harder in peak demand. Persistence is also required because the seller will not accept an offer first time. Offers may get turned down time and time again creating some personal criticism.

Virgin land is not a good investment. Although profit has been made investing in vacant land, the chance of earning any profit is slim. The owner must pay Spanish land tax, loan interest from a bank as mortgage lenders regard land mortgages as risky, and estate agency commission upon purchase. Most importantly there is a risk of the investment being worthless or money being tied up for a long period.

Land ownership is so risky that even builders try to avoid buying land until just before they start construction of a new development. Instead, builders buy options to purchase land, a neat financing trick that gives the builder control of the land with only a minimal cash investment until construction is ready to begin.

SUMMARY

♦ Estate agents know what is happening in the market-place and while they have commercial motives they can also be a valuable source of information. They do take high commissions.

♦ Always take legal advice when purchasing a property. Learn the procedures.

♦ There are no specific mortgages for buy-to-let in Spain. Mortgages can be in Sterling or in Euros, from British based companies in the UK, or with offices in Spain or Gibraltar, or from Spanish banks. A low interest rate Euro mortgage is considered to be the most appropriate unless seeking an 80%–100% loan based on the equity of an existing property.

♦ Allow 10% for legal costs when purchasing a Spanish property.

♦ As an investor, be unquestionably sharp when buying. Avoid land purchase.

8

Focusing on Letting Issues

WHAT MAKES A GOOD BUY-TO-LET?

Travelling time

Travel industry figures state that about 25% of all potential visitors to Spain will be deterred if it involves travelling for more than one hour from an airport at either end of their journey, and that if this time rises to one and a half hours it will deter around 50%. Travel convenience is therefore defined as less than one hour from an airport and while nothing can be done about the home location, the Spanish location is a letting and purchasing choice. This may well mean that some people do not leave home and Spanish rural cottages are difficult to let but the key criteria for renting is that the closer to a Spanish airport, the easier it is to find tenants.

Facilities

A holiday rental property should be located as close as possible to main attractions such as a beach and shopping facilities. For some tenants the proximity to a historic town, or the countryside would be a major asset, while for others it might be nightlife that is the main attraction. For families the two big theme parks, Terra Mitica at Benidorm or Universal Mediterrania at Tarragona, or one of the water parks are a focal point (see Appendix 5).

Having a property located close to activities such as golf, sailing, tennis, cycling and hiking can achieve rental income outside the high season. A property near to a golf course will not only have excellent views and lush greenery, but golfers who keep on coming all year round. A bonus of many golf courses is that they are near to a beautiful coast thus providing a double tenant market to aim for. Golf is booming, driven by tourism and the climate. The Costa del Sol is often referred to as Costa Del Golf, such is the profusion of new courses. They are carved out of barren landscapes, pampered and watered to produce lush green fairways. Holiday companies are always seeking properties for their golfing clients.

Convenience

Holiday tenants do not want to cook all the time. They want to eat out. A property will be much easier to let if it is within easy walking distance of shops, with a choice of bars and restaurants.

A swimming pool is necessary in some areas, as properties with pools are much easier to let than those without.

Some private letting agencies will not handle properties without a pool. Always hire a pool service to maintain the pool. Do not rely on tenants to do this. It is also possible in an apartment block to add value with a shared pool and a snazzy gym in the basement giving a tenant perceived convenience without leaving the premises.

Owner's possessions

A difficult judgement is deciding on the contents and standard of furnishing for a buy-to-let property. It can be argued that any standard of furnishing is permissible provided somebody is willing to pay the rent. But if letting through an agency, a holiday company or a Tourist Board, or positioning the letting 'up market', certain minimum standards must be met.

For a property to be attractive to paying tenants, the furniture and fittings should be comfortable and of good quality. The three most common complaints about holiday lettings are uncomfortable, poor quality beds, lack of kitchen equipment and lack of easy chairs.

A buy-to-let which is occupied by the owner should not have too many personal items lying around as personal possessions tend to clutter up properties so that tenants have nowhere to put their own bits and pieces. The problem of having a buy-to-let home that is liveable for the owner and at the same time lettable to others is one not easily solved. A home has a collection of the owner's personal favourite objects, which may make the tenant feel like an uncomfortable intruder.

Tenants actually want a let to look similar to a hotel room – clean, bland, no clutter, sterile and no personal traces of the owner which means the owner, when occupying the property, has to live like a tenant, so some of the fun of having a lettable property is lost.

TAKE CARE WITH...

Large tourist cities

Unfortunately tourist cities such as Benidorm have inherited a largely false image of a beer and chips resort, populated in summer by crowds of flabby, middle-aged people otherwise known as the British abroad. Everybody knows that holidaymakers go to Benidorm for the climate, for the clean and safe streets, for the beaches, for the good food, for the excellent service and for the pleasant company! It's worth remembering that 80% of the residents of Benidorm and 50% of its holidaymakers are Spanish. For the City Council, taking care of five million tourists a year, it is a serious business and they are determined to bury this image ... but will they? For Benidorm also read Torremolinos and Maspalomas. The locations are different but the picture is similar.

They are not places for a buy-to-let investor where hotels and packaged tourists dominate the scene.

Valencia's Ley Reguladora de Actividad Urbanistica

The Valencian regional law regulating urban development was passed in 1994 with the aim of stimulating urban development. Many parts of the region were caught in a situation where normal urban growth was paralysed by a maze of holdings whose owners refused to sell or to participate in development projects. Town planners found their projects blocked by stubborn people. As a result the rationalisation of streets, sewage, lighting systems and parks required for harmonious urban growth could not go ahead.

To deal with this situation, the regional government came up with new rules. The legislation provides for compulsory participation by landowners in development projects backed by Town Halls, and ensures that existing owners do not benefit from windfall profits.

These profits occur when an owner in the path of development discovers his formerly rural farm is about to become a city block. The land is suddenly worth a fortune. Paying for this however, formerly fell to the owner's fellow taxpayers. So the Valencian authorities designed a way to make the landowners pay their share.

The Town Hall involved can plan and carry out an urbanisation project on its own, or it can designate a private developer as the 'urbanising agent'. The latter is the most common. This delegated private developer then acts as an agent of the municipal authority, with the right to take private land or compel payment for it even when the owner does not wish to sell.

But in some areas the owners of houses on very large grounds, many of them established for 20 years or more, are facing an invasion of developers building modestly priced houses on small plots. And what makes it worse is that they are being asked to pay for the privilege under the terms of the law as the urbanising agent will only pay a fraction of the market value of the land.

This is clearly not what it was designed for. Buy-to-let investors have to take care with this Valencian law but there is now a determination to make the authorities in London, Brussels, Madrid and Valencia more aware of the situation and to demand modifications. This will happen because the present situation is intolerable.

TENANT MARKETS

The vast majority of lettings in Spain are for holiday lets in coastal areas and business lets in major and provincial cities. Having said that, this is neither an exclusive statement nor the end of the matter, for certain inland university cities are visited by tourists and also have business and student letting opportunities. But it certainly helps to identify a type of tenant in order to keep advertising costs down or to keep a letting agency on track. To match a property to possible clientele it is better to target one market.

Friends and family

A predetermined position should be established with letting to friends and family. If not running a business it can be very tempting to let to someone you know rather than a complete stranger since there is an expectation that the property will be well looked after. When renting to family and friends the owner has to learn how to raise the delicate issue of payment. Since there are no marketing costs and management costs, a lower price can be offered while still generating as much income as would have been obtained through a letting agency. This arrangement keeps everyone happy. It can however end in tears if the friend overstays the welcome period, or does not make a contribution to costs, and has to be politely encouraged to leave.

Holiday letting

A property that is let for holiday purposes, whether or not you live in it yourself for part of the year, generally speaking requires certain services to be provided such as cleaning and changes of bed linen. Holiday letting imposes a greater workload on the owner than any other form of letting. The amount paid by the holidaymaker will normally include an allowance for utility usage of gas, electricity and water. Holiday letting demand may be seasonal, but there are often people looking for short-term winter breaks who prefer a fully equipped home to a hotel.

Business people

Business executives, people in the entertainment profession, doctors and nurses, contract workers and visiting academics are examples of people who might require a property to rent. Tenants such as these are excellent, blue chip occupants. They are busy professionals, high earners, working all day, who are accustomed to high standards. These lets command a 25% premium for that type of property. The rent can be paid or guaranteed by the company.

The greatest demand is for studios and one bedroom apartments in a city environment, as tenants are mostly single people rather than families. Although a number of business let landlords are people letting their own property temporarily, by far the biggest number of owners are investment landlords, who are prepared to go that bit further than the absolute basics and provide a few touches of luxury for good clients.

Students

Students like to share flats or houses. Although student accommodation is less classy than that offered to professionals, it still has to offer the basics. Students only want to take a property for nine months of the year, which is a problem for the landlord as it is unoccupied for the rest of the time. Money can be made from letting to students, particularly in Spain's many university towns. The rent is guaranteed by confirmation that this person is a genuine student, and references are from parents, who act as guarantors.

What sort of tenant do you really want?

Given a free choice, all tenants should be people in full-time paid employment. Concerns about payment are therefore reduced. Artists, struggling writers and musicians of any kind do not make good tenants. Some landlords discriminate too against people with things such as tattoos, men with ponytails, and anyone with lots of body piercing, as these can be characteristics of low paying potential. It is not legal to discriminate on grounds of race.

A position is also required to be taken over children and pets. Some properties are suitable for either, some luxury properties suitable for neither, but conversely some landlords welcome both as it does widen the tenant pool.

Do not bargain with a potential tenant over the rent. Wait for a full-rate paying tenant than someone who wants to negotiate down. Rental agencies advise against this, saying that it is better to have a lower-paying tenant than no tenant at all; but of course agencies are inclined to grab their commission.

SUMMARY

◆ A good buy-to-let has to offer convenience, best defined as being close to a Spanish airport, close to desirable attractions and close to shops and restaurants. An added value extra such as a swimming pool is a bonus.

◆ For tenant and owner to share a property at different times, the owner has to live like a tenant. Some of the fun can be lost.

◆ Avoid large tourist cities as they have poor letting potential.

◆ While the current Valencian law is still in place take care when buying on the fringes of the countryside in the Costa Blanca.

◆ Define and stick to a single tenant market. Be clear about the type of tenant you really want.

9

Marketing Your Property

CONSUMER CHOICE

Faced with an ever-growing choice of rental products to choose from, how do owners know that their property is desirable to tenants and how do they go about renting it out? And of course, the burning question – how can the owner ensure maximum return from the rental? There are many agents in Spain who will advertise property, there are many tour operators who would like to rent out a property too, but the owner may choose to market it personally, thus cutting out the middleman.

A good exercise is to search the Internet under the heading of 'villa and apartment rentals' – followed by the name of a village, town, city, region or island in Spain. This will lead to some advertised rental properties in the chosen search area. In some cases there may be considerable competition but do not be overwhelmed by the deluge of information.

This simple search will show that the market for holiday villas in Spain encompasses low rated houses, middle of the range and a few select exclusive properties. The majority of tour operators – who pay high rental rates – cater to the middle market of mass tourism and no longer accept a property that is below average. The standard is getting higher.

Remember, whatever letting method is utilised, it has to be someone you can trust. It may be trust in your own judgement in going it alone, or trust in a letting agent or a tour operator or trust that your property will be returned in good condition. Whatever it is, look for this feeling of trust.

DO IT YOURSELF

Doing it yourself simply means spending time and money advertising, preparing brochures, making contacts and utilising the internet. Sounds simple but unless you let people know about the property the business will never materialise. The trend in letting is away from traditional advertising, such as newspapers and magazines, towards the internet and although this new technology is cheaper, totally abandoning conventional advertising is unwise (see Figure 11).

Advertising in newspapers

UK national newspapers, particularly those with weekend holiday sections, can gain access to a high readership at short notice with regularly placed, small advertisements.

Figure 11. Do it yourself rental marketing.

It can however be an expensive form of advertising. An information pack is usually available from the newspaper, which includes readership profiles, making it possible to deduce if the people reading the newspaper match the profile of potential tenants. Combining a small advertisement with a reference to a web address is often the most cost effective advertising method for a small buy-to-let investor.

English language, weekly Spanish newspapers have a role to play in finding tenants who are already in Spain, wishing to rent while looking for a property to buy or waiting for one to be built.

Magazines
Special interest magazines, targeted at customers who undertake golfing, sailing, hiking and other activities are

often a better media than newspapers. They have a longer shelf life than newspapers but they also have longer publication lead times. There are also companies producing directories of properties let directly by owners. The owner pays for the advertisement and handles the bookings personally. Some directories have changed from producing brochures to being web based.

Brochures

An advert, or even a website, should be backed up by a brochure. Personal computers, colour printers and good software have revolutionised 'do it yourself' brochure design. Think carefully about the design and the quality of printing that can be achieved. Use photographs of the interior, the exterior and local area tourist spots. Use a logo on letterheads and envelopes. The professional brochure includes important details such as the exact location, local attractions, details of how to get there with a map and the name, address and telephone number of a local contact.

The Internet

There has been major growth in the number of bookings and enquiries made over the Internet, with a corresponding fall in the number of bookings taken through traditional media. It can be a very cost effective option for operators, particularly small operators who find traditional advertising media expensive. A well-designed website can supply as much, and usually more information than a brochure. It can be done faster, at a time convenient to the customer without waiting for a brochure to arrive in the post. The up-to-the-minute information contains details of availability and the latest prices. Although computer penetration is as high in Spain as anywhere else, always remember that not everyone has the confidence to make an internet booking.

Such is the growth of the internet as a media information service it can be effective at a number of different levels. The number of replies is a simple equation of 'cost versus hits'. Some different examples of internet advertising are given below:

www.brittany-ferries.com	A large well known holiday company that appears on many websites.
www.privatevillas.co.uk	Owners advertise their properties on this site, which is backed up by magazine promotion.
www.holiday-rentals.co.uk	A very large site.
www.ownersdirect.co.uk	Another large site.
www.holidaybank.com	A large domain site for holiday companies and individual property rentals. The holiday companies may be no more than a local agency offering a letting, maintenance and cleaning service for a group of properties in one area.

www.simplyspanish.com   A localised property sales and letting company.

Personal contacts

Personal contacts are one of the best means of marketing a property. If the buy-to-let is to be used for a considerable time by the owner and it is only to be let for, say, 20 weeks each year, it only takes ten lettings at two weeks each to achieve this. Friends and family, work contacts and information cards in the local area may do the trick.

Queries

Planning to let a home personally will necessitate a system to deal with enquiries about such things as flights and car rentals. It is easier to let clients do it themselves, but the owner should be able to offer good advice and be able put them in touch with airlines, ferry companies, travel agents and car rental companies.

CHOOSING LETTING AGENTS

The advantage of using a letting agency is that they put some distance between the owner and the tenant; they handle references, inventories, deposits and direct debits and they can intervene if disputes arise. No spare time? Then use an agent, who will take care of everything and save the time and expense of advertising and finding clients. It also makes sense to use an agency if the Buy to Let investor lives a long way from the property or if it is a specialised property likely to command a high rental.

No agent can magically produce a tenant. Agencies can do their best, but they cannot create tenants where a market does not exist. They cannot guarantee that there will be no void periods. If an owner finds tenants for holiday letting then all the paid rent is retained, but using a letting agency will cost at least 12.5%, if not more, of the agreed rental in commission. The charges rise with any increased service offered, with 20%–25% charged for rental and cleaning of holiday lets and up to 35% for a total management package of:

♦ A letting service.

♦ Emergency property maintenance and repair.

♦ Day-to-day management of guests' laundry, property cleaning and post collection.

♦ Personal assistance for tenants, guests and visitors to include collection from the airport, car hire and language translation.

♦ Arranging insurances to cover property, contents and personal health.

♦ A legal and fiscal service to cover the payment of bills and annual tax returns.

Long-term letting charges are similar at around 12.5% with an additional fee for introducing tenants and drawing up agreements.

Always choose a letting agent with care. They should have a separate client account that cannot be raided to keep their business going. Use a specialist letting agency, rather than an estate agent who has a letting business as a sideline. Where lettings are their only concern, they have to work harder otherwise they have no business.

Match the agency to the type of property being let. If students are the market, use an agency specialising in this type of letting. For corporate clients, choose a market leader for this kind of rental. Up-market properties need up-market agencies and vice versa. Be aware that some agents do not permit owners to use their own property during peak-letting season.

HOLIDAY TOUR OPERATORS

Quality properties with swimming pools in holiday resorts are in demand by holiday tour companies. Some tour operators like to work only with an established agent. This way they do not have to deal with individual owners. The agent handles everything on behalf of the owner. It can be worthwhile asking an agent to do all the work – providing services such as cleaning and laundry maintenance – and let him take his commission. This is easier for tour operators also because all problems can be reported to this agent, rather than chasing up individual owners.

Other tour operators will work directly with owners, saving money by not going through an agent to obtain a property. If a good working rapport can be established between the owner and the tour operator then this usually works in favour of both parties, as a property owner will provide a better maintenance service than an agent. If living close to the property being let and willing to receive calls from the tour operator regarding maintenance, repairs and questions that may occur, then it is in the owner's interest to work directly with the tour operator.

In either case agree all points about maintenance, bills, pool cleaning, house cleaning and suchlike in the contract. Know who is responsible for what payments. If the maintenance is through an agent, it is advisable to get them to check before they call for expensive plumbers and electricians.

Tour operators who look after the clients and the property often employ holiday representatives. They can prove invaluable in spotting things such as clients leaving the air-conditioning or the outside lights switched on all day. The representative can also advise clients about how to use appliances within the villa, and help prevent break-ages, ensuring some peace of mind for the owner.

There are two agreements that are commonly made between the owner and the tour operator. The property can be handed over with a contract that states a guaranteed payment which is calculated beforehand, written into the contract and paid even if the property is not rented fully, or even if it remains empty. Alternatively, a second option is to rent out the property on an *ad hoc* basis, but there will only be payment when there are bookings.

If the property is fully booked there is greater potential to receive more money with the *ad hoc* arrangement and greater flexibility for the owner to use the property.

Usually with a guaranteed payment system, the property is only for the use of the tour operator's clients. A property under the control of only one holiday company is the better arrangement as it is in their interest to ensure everything is in good condition for their clients.

CONTRACT OF LETTING – OWNER/AGENT

The agreement between the owner and an agent or tour operator is called a *Contrato de Encargo de Appensmiento* (Contract of Letting). One such contract (outlined in Appendix 3) refers to a property in Spain governed by Spanish law and is normally written in Spanish with an additional English translation.

COMING TO TERMS WITH GROSS INCOME

So how much money can be expected for a rental? Or put another way, how much will the client pay, since the deductions from the gross payment are dependent on the marketing arrangements.

Holiday lettings

- The basic price for a holiday apartment close to the Mediterranean, or on one of the islands is 460 Euros per week high season for one bedroom accommodation. A two bedroom apartment 540 Euros per week, a 3 bedroom 630 Euros, 4 bedroom 710 Euros, and a five bedroom 975 Euros.

- A small holiday bedsit in an apartment block, will only fetch around 150 Euros per week.

- A top of the range detached villa with swimming pool, close to all facilities with all mod cons, will command 1,250 Euros to 1,500 Euros per week high season. A mid-range detached villa will fetch 900 Euros per week high season.

- Moving inland, a large farmhouse in Andalucia will cost 600 Euros per week, a town house in the mountains 300 Euros per week.

- In premium coastal locations prices can be 30% greater.

- Conversely, for longer lettings of several months, discounts of at least 50% are normal bringing holiday letting costs in line with long-term rental prices.

- Mid season and low season rates are approximately 75% and 50% of high season rates respectively.

- It should be noted that some holiday organisations are now offering a car in the basic rental package.

Longer-term city lettings

- Longer-term city lets to business clients and students can vary enormously. They do not command the same high prices as holiday lets but attract tenants for 52 weeks per year.

- Cheap, build to rent apartments in skyscraper blocks in Barcelona only command 125 Euros per week. The same figure can also be the basic price for a small property in a rural location with no strong attractions or facilities.

- A bottom of the range, long-term let bedsit apartment in any location, can fall to 70 Euros per week.

- Where individually appointed apartments are available in provincial cities, inland or on the coast, they command 200 Euros per week or more which is much the same as a 60% discount on a basic two bedroom holiday apartment.

HOW TO BE A GOOD LANDLORD

What are the characteristics of a good landlord? Someone who provides good value accommodation! Someone who would be happy to live in the accommodation being let! A good landlord gives the customer a satisfactory product. It is all part of marketing.

Local information

The owner's approach to holiday lettings is important. After all it is a fun-filled fortnight! The clients want to start their holiday on arrival. They have planned it for some time. For a quick assimilation of the important facts an information pack should be provided for clients explaining how things work, security systems, what not to do, where to shop, recommended restaurants, local emergency numbers and health services such as doctors, hospitals and dentists. A visitors' book where customers can write their comments and recommendations is a standard Spanish practice.

A free grocery pack with a bottle of wine to greet them on their arrival is a little touch that may ensure repeat business and some recommendations. After all, word of mouth advertising is the cheapest and always the best.

Offer a clean rental

If the property is clean when a tenant moves in, the chances are very good that it will be clean when the tenant moves out. Scruffy properties take far longer to rent, command a low price and attract the wrong sort of tenant. A good tenant simply will not accept a rental that is a mess. They will not want to spend time cleaning. They know they are good tenants, they know they can find a clean place, and they will skip an unclean property.

Utility bills

Utilities expenses such as electricity, water, gas, telephone and heating fuel, are another inevitable form of expense. These may be partly the responsibility of a long-term tenant but not of a holiday tenant. There is nothing wrong with this unless you live in an arid area of Spain and have a big garden that takes a lot of expensive water. Do not expect any tenant to go out of his or her way to pay a big water bill to keep plants and flowers alive. The answer is a water allowance. It does not have to be much. It does not even have to equal the costs. It is just the idea that the landlord is contributing.

If the property has a pool, a pool maintenance service is a must. Never rely on a tenant to take care of a pool.

Rent for less

It is important not to be penny-wise and pound-foolish when setting rental rates. The foolish landlord always tries to get top price for a property. The wise landlord rents for just below the market price. The reasoning is simple – to get top price you have to wait for a tenant. If you rent just below the market, the property will let quicker.

If you are letting a property where the market is 1,000 Euros a month and you put it up for 970 Euros you lose 30 Euros a month because you are renting below market. At the end of a year it will mean a loss of 360 Euros. All else being equal, tenants will choose this property first over similar properties renting at 1,000 Euros. Now consider the landlord who insists on 1,000 Euros a month. Assuming that the market value is correct, he will get it. But it might take a month until he finds a tenant. He will lose 1,000 Euros of potential rent during that month. Is it better to lose 360 Euros or 1,000 Euros?

Do not delay fixing a problem
When you become a landlord you also assume the duties of a 'fix-it' person. You are expected to take care of all the little as well as the big things that go wrong. This includes fixing leaky toilets, blocked drains, sprinkler systems that don't turn on and light switches that don't work. What's more, you're expected to fix these things quickly. If the property is not maintained how can you expect the tenant to do it for you? They are going to take their cue from the owner. If you don't care about the property, they won't either; and if you let them get away with running your property into the ground, they will take advantage of it.

SUMMARY
- The consumer is faced with a bewildering choice of holiday rentals.

- It is possible to market a property personally by advertising, brochures, word of mouth or by using the Internet.

- There are many different methods of advertising through the internet.

- Letting agents are useful if the owner lives far away or 'wishes to wash their hands' of the property. No agent, no matter how good, can guarantee 100% bookings. A specialist agency should be chosen to attract specialist clientele.

- Premium properties in tourist areas are best marketed through tour operators. They give high rents, good tenants and peace of mind.

- City properties of an individual nature are also good earners.

- Learn to be a good landlord.

Running a Business

LETTING CONTRACTS

Holiday contracts

A holiday tenant, renting a property from a company or a person in, say, England, France or Germany will have a contract written in the language of that country, signed before leaving on holiday. This is perfectly acceptable. The contract should make provision for terms and conditions associated with a holiday letting, covering statements on the following:

♦ Payments: it is usual to request a deposit to secure a booking – usually a percentage paid in advance, with the balance payable at some specified date before arrival.

- Cancellation: people should be encouraged to take out holiday cancellation insurance.

- Policy statements on who may not be welcome, e.g. children, pets, and single-sex groups.

- Bed linen, table linen, towels – provision and charging.

- Facilities for children: cots, highchairs, and fireguards.

- Smoking policy.

- Guests' responsibility for their own belongings and cars.

- Arrival and departure times.

- Breakages and damages policy.

Temporada contracts

Short-term contracts are called *Arrienda de Temporada*. The straightforward, standard contract is written in Spanish and normally in the native tongue of the tenant. It is for a period of up to one year although most are for much less than that. Properties let this way are furnished and the contract should include a detailed inventory of contents with a returnable deposit required to cover any damages caused by the temporary tenant. The contract is for a specific period of time at a stated price. The renewal of the contract is only at the agent or landlord's discretion. An example of this type of contract is given in Appendix 4 and a standard form is available from some *tabacs* (state-owned tobacco shops that provide stamps and forms).

Vivienda contracts

The contract for a long-term rental is called *Arrienda de Vivienda*. The law provides for long-term rentals to be of up to five years duration thus giving the tenant a degree of security. If the landlord offers a contract of three years duration, which is accepted, and then the tenant wishes to stay on for another two years it is automatically renewed on the same terms. If the tenant leaves after three years as arranged, then the contract is terminated. Annual rent increases, in line with inflation, take place during the contracted term. A new level of rent is set at the commencement of a new contract. Towards the end of a five-year *Vivienda* contract the landlord is obliged to notify the tenant officially by a notarised letter. If the landlord does not notify the tenant officially, the contract can be renewed for two years at the same rent.

Which contract?

It is important to determine at the outset if a holiday letting contract, short-term letting or long-term letting is being asked or offered. Legal advisors in Spain struggle to write individual *Vivienda* contracts because of their complexity and a need to cover every eventuality. They often advise the issue of successive *Temporada* contracts for a letting of more than one year, thus bypassing some tenant rights. In this case the lawyer is taking advantage of the tenant, denying him the right to a longer contract, and leaving the way open for rent increases beyond the level of inflation at the end of the year. Some tenants simply accept this practice, but others get legal advice and go to court. The tenant declares that he signed a one-year *Temporada* contract, he or she lives and works there, it is home, and asks the court to order the contract to be extended to the full five years. In many cases, the court has ruled in favour of the tenant.

The Law lays down the basic structure of rental contracts but they can vary in detail. It is important to obtain legal advice prior to offering or signing a *Temporada* or *Vivienda* contract and to make sure everything is understood. Community charges and local taxes are the responsibility of the owner and an allowance for this may be included in the rent but not added as an extra. No matter the length of time a property is let it is the landlord who is a member of any *Comunidad* (the owner of a community property with shared common elements).

OBEYING THE RULES

The regulation of tourist accommodation is a matter for each *Comunidad*. This effectively means that tourist accommodation laws vary throughout Spain with the hot spots in the Costas and Islands receiving a number of directives. It is perfectly proper for the Spanish authorities to regulate accommodation in this manner, ensuring that visitors are not overcharged and the facilities are of a recognised standard. Pacos' house in the country, should he choose to rent it, may be suitable for him and his family but viewed from a northern European perspective it may well be insanitary. Enter the regulation of tourist accommodation with minimum standards.

As an example the Valencian government asks that owners register their tourist accommodation with the Tourist Board. It may be in the city, a metropolitan area or in the country. It may be a simple property let out for a few weeks a year, a bed and breakfast, a guesthouse or a hotel. Either way it has to be registered if utilised for one day or 52 weeks per year. Over one year, which of course in letting terms is a *Vivienda* contract, free market forces apply with no registration necessary.

The registration and classification of letting accommodation appears to offer the buy-to-let investor few advantages since a copy of the ten-page application goes to the tax authorities. As a consequence people conveniently ignore it. With a letting property in a city, or an up-market villa on the coast available for a few weeks a year this may be an acceptable risk, since the one advantage of having the property listed at the local tourist office as letting accommodation is an inappropriate marketing tool. These properties are unlikely to infringe any minimum standard and policing from the Tourist Board is a waste of their time.

In rural areas however a different set of circumstances apply. Money is at stake here and most letting property is registered with the Tourist Board. A property is classified as a *casa rural* coming under the headings of a shared or non-shared rural house or a tourist hostel for group use. The majority of casa rural accommodation has been reformed and equipped to provide quality conditions with the assistance of grant aid. Properties respect the environment in which they are located, and are usually built to traditional architecture and design using classical materials such as stone and wood. Advertising of letting accommodation is through the Tourist Board in high-class publications.

Casa rural accommodation has a minimum:

◆ Hot water in kitchens and bathrooms.

◆ One full bathroom for every six beds.

◆ Lamps, power points and heating in all rooms and communal areas.

◆ Water supplies and electricity.

◆ Effective elimination systems for solid refuse and waste water.

◆ Fire extinguisher and first aid kits.

◆ A recognised quality seal such as ISO 9000.

If renting out a property as holiday accommodation throughout the year and providing services such as bed and breakfast, then the property must be registered irrespective of location. This means that inspectors will be obliged to come and carry out an assessment of the standards including food preparation.

There is another important distinction. A small buy-to-let investor will have the revenue from letting taxed in the normal way, as income, but the registration of a business with a significant turnover is an altogether different matter (see Chapter 11 on taxation). The Valencian rules can be seen at: www.comunidad-valenciana.org/ordenacion/ menu.

When letting an apartment it is also necessary to check that this is permitted under the community rules.

Additional regulations apply in the Balearics and Canary Islands where letting is not encouraged. It may also be necessary to notify the property insurance company.

EVICTION AND COMPLAINTS

Eviction

Under what conditions can the owner regain his property and evict the tenant? Failure to pay the rent, damage to the property, using the property for immoral purposes, subletting unless agreed in the contract and causing a serious nuisance to the neighbours are some obvious reasons. But in all cases a court order must be obtained against the tenant and many months will pass before eviction.

Although the contract and law state a rental period is finished, a landlord will have difficulty evicting someone who chooses to stay. Again a court order is necessary but the procedure will take some time.

The most common abuse takes place with holiday rentals where tenants have signed up for one month and then simply remain in the property without paying any further rent. Four to six months later, the landlord is able to obtain an eviction order, but the tenants have lived rent-free for that period. The court will issue a judgement against them for the amount of rent owed but by then they will simply have moved on.

Complaints

Occasionally a landlord may have to deal with a complaint from a tenant. Acknowledge, investigate, make a decision, reply and take remedial action if applicable. If it is valid, put matters right, informing the tenant and giving an expected timescale. Otherwise, state no action is required and give the reasons.

Complaints may come from sources other than a tenant. In fact they may be about the tenants. Serious complaints may require consultation with a legal representative before proceeding.

A tenant of a holiday property can also complain to the tourist office in the province or town where the property is located, provided the property has been registered as tourist accommodation in the first place. The tourist office will often side with the landlord provided all the necessary procedures have been adhered to. Complaints from longer-term tenants are usually addressed to the *Oficina Municipal de Informacion al Consumidor*, which is the consumer information office, directed by regional government to deal with consumer problems such as rent.

WRITING A BUSINESS PLAN

It makes good sense to write a business plan. It will probably not be required for a mortgage but think about preparing one anyway as it forces a thought process about the business and the marketplace. A plan will also cover the business objectives, the customers and how they will be reached, financial planning including both profit and cash flow, competitor analysis, business risks and sensitivities. A business plan should be realistic and not over-optimistic. Remember that most businesses fail because they run out of cash, as profits are slower to materialise than expected. Readers can see a business plan together with the financial statements and ratios for Case Study – Castles in the Air in Appendix 6.

KEEPING THE BOOKS

Buying a property, wheeling and dealing, even dealing with tenants and maintenance can be an enjoyable challenge. Accounting, on the other hand, is just plain work. However there is no point in making money if it cannot be recorded. How fast is it coming in and where it is going on its way out? Since no one enjoys accounting any more than anyone else try to keep it simple. Do not spend any more time on it than is absolutely necessary as bookkeeping itself does not make money – it just helps to keep track of it.

Capital gains and trading profit

The financial increase occurring between the buying and selling price of a property is called a capital gain and may well play a significant part in assessing the overall financial success of a buy-to-let investment. Trading profit is a separate issue – rental income will be received from which operating expenses must be deducted thus giving a trading profit.

If running a formal business, it is important to keep trading profit and capital gains separate for accounting purposes, regarding a capital gain as a bonus only when realised. However for a small Buy to Let investor with only one property, who is not required to submit formal accounts, they may be considered together.

Balance sheets and cash flow

A balance sheet is a report at a fixed point in time – usually at the end of the financial year – stating the assets and liabilities of the business. Keeping a positive cash flow by constant reference to the bank balance is one of the main criteria during a start up phase of a business. It is possible for a business to make a profit but to run out of cash.

Depreciation

Any owner of a registered business may deduct an allowance on tax returns for the theoretical loss in value of furniture and fittings due to the passage of time. Depreciation is an allowable income tax deduction to compensate the owner for losses in value caused by wear, tear and obsolescence of fittings of value. A small Buy to Let investor should also show depreciation in accounts and cash flow statements in order to give a true reflection of the rental.

Although there are several methods most people prefer the conservative straight-line depreciation method because it is the easiest to use and it gives easily predictable results rather than the annually changing results of accelerated methods. To use the straight-line depreciation method, the asset is divided by its estimated useful life in years. The result is its annual depreciation deduction. So for example, the furniture and fittings of a tenanted property that cost 10,000 Euros, with an average life of ten years, will result in a depreciation charge of 1,000 Euros per year.

Expenses

Knowing rental income is important, but knowing rental expenses can be even more important. These may be:

- Advertising costs.
- Mortgage repayments – if any.
- Agency letting costs.
- Property and Contents Insurance.
- Depreciation of furniture and fittings.
- Maintenance and decoration costs.
- Utility charges.
- Administrative expenses.
- Cleaning, gardening and pool service.
- Taxes.

Property insurance will ordinarily cover fire and content losses. Policies can be obtained to provide some special type of protection, such as flood insurance. Also liability insurance can be obtained to provide protection against claims for damages suffered by individuals using the property. Administrative expenses will include outlays for accounting and legal services.

Maintenance and repairs are two major expense items for most tenanted properties. In this category are included interior and exterior repairs of various kinds, such as plumbing, electrical, heating systems, and repairs to appliances. Also included are exterior painting and other requirements. The distinction between repairs, improvements and makeovers is not always clear-cut.

BUSINESS RATIOS

Rent/Price ratio

A Buy to Let property should, as a minimum, be rented for enough money to pay the expenses. Can this be realistically done? In truth, it can be difficult. The rent/price ratio is a rule of thumb that wise investors use to gauge the relationship between monthly rental income and the price of the property. It simply says that the monthly income from rents should be around 1% of the total purchase price. In the UK, Building Societies have another similar rule for Buy to Let investors – income should be 125% to 150% of borrowings.

Yield and Return

Once the property is purchased, up and running, the two most important ratios are the Yield and Return which will give an indication of the profit that is being achieved on the investment. The profit figure is less all expenses. With Yield the capital figure is the current value of the property and with Return it is the value of the owner's investment on the bottom line. Which one to use? The return is probably more appropriate and the resultant figure should be greater than any comparative investment!

$$\text{Yield} = \text{Profit} \div \text{Capital value of the property} \times 100$$
$$\text{Return} = \text{Profit} \div \text{Owner's investment} \times 100$$

Expense ratio

When running a business a starting point for reviewing operating expenses is to examine the figures in as much detail as is possible. One widely used comparative expense measure is the percentage that total operating expenses represent of gross possible income (that is, gross income at full occupancy).

$$\text{Expense ratio} = \text{Total operating expenses} \div \text{Gross possible income} \times 100$$

The expense ratio will tend to vary with the type of property and its age. A general pattern usually observed is that the older the building, the higher the percentage of income that will be claimed by operating expenses, while new buildings tend to have a honeymoon period (see Figure 12).

Age of property (years)	Maintenance costs (% of rental income)
0–10	5%
10–25	10%
25+	15%

Figure 12. Maintenance costs versus age of property.

Gross income multiplier
If the Buy to Let is unsuccessful, or for some other reason has to be sold, the gross income multiplier (GIM) relates the current gross income of the property to its purchase price.

$$\text{Gross Income Multiplier} = \text{Purchase price} \div \text{Current gross income}$$

The GIM is a technique that can be used to appraise the value of an income-producing property. The procedure used is to multiply the current gross income of the property by the GIM to determine an estimate of the market value for the property being appraised.

Market price $=$ GIM $\times$ Current gross income.

This technique is a rule of thumb not unlike the price/earnings ratio (P/E ratio) used in share value analysis, where one measure of the value of a common stock is found by multiplying an appropriate P/E ratio by the current earnings per share. It is also similar to the rent/price ratio which is used prior to buying.

BUSINESS IS BUSINESS

Renting property is not democracy in action. It is a business. It is important for the owner to strike the right tone in a relationship with a tenant, letting agent or tour operator. It should not be arbitrary or dictatorial. The customer may always be correct but the owner has to be in charge and how the tenant, agent or tour operator is handled will largely determine what happens to the property.

The owner sets the tone. The tone may vary depending on the tenant market. If the business is well run, it will be because the owner knows how to run it smoothly and how to communicate a clear set of guidelines and expectations. Let people know what is to be done for them and what is expected of them in return.

What tenants are told about a property is part of an education programme. Some landlords want their tenants to know that they are dealing with a large, powerful concern. In some cases, the landlords do not even want the tenant to know who the owners are. They prefer to have the tenants think they are dealing with a management company. This way there is an organised management programme and the tenants have to fit into it. Everyone gets treated the same way. Other landlords want their clients to know they are dealing with a friendly individual who will look after all their needs at the drop of a hat, particularly if they are paying top dollar for a luxury villa with a pool in summer season.

Setting the tone in any business involves dealing with people. Property problems are almost invariably people problems. Apartments do not break their own windows or doors. Buildings do not draw on the walls, or put holes in the carpets. Tenants do not do this either, unless they think that they can get away with it.

Properties do not cause problems. Buildings just sit there, quietly minding their own business. Sure, houses and other types of property are quite capable of producing anxiety. Roofs leak, sewer and other plumbing lines break, paint wears out and lawns need periodic cutting. Then there are fires, floods, blizzards, earthquakes, tornadoes, hurricanes and all the other possible calamities beyond the property owner's control. But tenants are the main source of problems that an owner will encounter.

SUMMARY
- There are three letting contracts. The *Arrienda de Vivienda* is a difficult contract to write to cover all eventualities.

- Eviction is only by court order.

- In many *Comunidads* property for letting has to be registered with the local Tourist Board.

- Try to understand accounts and business ratios but remember they do not in themselves make profit, but only record it and perhaps give an indication of what is right or wrong.

- Letting is a business and the owner sets the tone. Do not be overwhelmed by agents, tour operators and tenants. Educate them!

- It is people who cause problems, not buildings!

How Much Tax Will You Pay?

UNDERSTANDING PERSONAL TAXATION

Personal taxation is complicated at the best of times. Also, as you would expect, the tax system is constantly changing. Most taxes in Spain are based on self-assessment where the individual is liable to report and calculate any tax due. Since we all have difficulty doing this, the average new resident or non resident, grappling with the language of the Spanish tax system has little chance of getting this correct. Enter the *gestor* who will not only perform these administrative tasks but may even suggest legitimate methods of tax avoidance.

A *gestor* acts as an intermediary between Spanish officialdom and the general public, being a registered agent dealing with government departments. It says much about the Spanish way of life that such a person is necessary to deal with its wearisome bureaucracy. *Gestors* are well respected. They are competent, highly qualified administrators. What do they do? For the Spanish they simply deal with the complicated mass of paperwork. For foreigners they do the same, particularly with taxation. It is important to note that a resident with only one Spanish property may make a declaration personally but if they own two or more properties then a qualified tax adviser, such as a *gestor*, has to make the declaration on the owner's behalf.

Spain is not a tax haven. Its level of taxation is, however, generally low. The *Agencia Estatal de Administracion Tributaria* collects government taxes but it is commonly called by its old name, *Hacienda*. The Spanish tax year is 1 January to 31 December. Tax returns must be presented between the 1 May and the 20 June.

A non resident spends less than six months per year in Spain. A Spanish resident is one who spends more than six months per year in the country, who has a *Residencia* and has notified the tax authorities back home of his or her departure on form P85. This triggers entry into the Spanish tax system, which has a treaty with other European countries designed to ensure income already taxed in one country is not taxed again in another.

To complete a full tax return, some documentation is necessary.

◆ Details of an *Numero de Identificacion de Extranjero* (NIE) number, address, age and marital status.

- Proof of income.

- A year-end bank statement showing interest paid and average balance.

- A recent *Impuesto sobre Bienes Inmuebles* statement (known as **IBI** – local rates).

- Details of mortgages, sale or purchase of any property, the cost of any home extension.

- Receipts for any tax paid in another country.

- Details of any changes in stocks, shares, investments, insurance policies, major assets and artefacts.

There are five main taxes administered by the *Hacienda* which a resident and non resident will have to deal with:

- Property taxes.

- Income tax (*Impusto sobre la renta de las personas fisicas*).

- Capital gains tax.

- Wealth tax (*impuesto sobre el patrimonio*).

- Inheritance tax (*impuesto sobre sucesiones y donaciones*).

Property taxes

A non resident is liable for *Patrimonio and Renta* taxes (wealth tax and unearned income tax). *Patrimonio* is calculated at 0.2% of either the property value as declared in the *Escritura*, the rateable value or the market value, whichever is higher. *Renta* is nothing to do with renting out the property. It is a separate tax that is paid with the *Patrimonio*, calculated as 25% of 1.1% of the rateable value of a property. It is a little bit complicated but to give an approximation allow 0.5% of the property value each year for both taxes.

One important point however! A resident with only one property does not pay the *Patrimonio* or *Renta* taxes but does so on the second and subsequent properties.

Although not classified as an income tax both residents and non residents will pay *Impuesto de Bienes Inmuebles* (IBI) which are local taxes or rates, to the local Town Hall, usually amounting to 0.5%–0.7% of the rateable value of a property (*catastro*) assessed by the rates office and based on the square metres of land, house, pool, garage and the age of the property. In some areas an additional charge is levied as a rubbish removal tax (*Exaciones Municipales Basura*).

Income tax – non resident

It is quite legal for either a resident or non resident property owner in Spain to rent out a property. The fundamental rule is that the rental income must be declared for Spanish income tax. If the tenant pays in Pounds or Euros before leaving for a holiday property in Spain, legally this income arises in Spain because the property is in Spain. It may well be the case that owners who casually let their property will say nothing about it to the tax authorities, and the chances of getting caught are slim. Nevertheless, Spanish income tax is due on any income arising in Spain. A non resident is liable for Spanish income tax of 25% of rental income.

Income tax – resident

Income tax is payable on both earned and unearned worldwide income such as wages, pensions, property and investment income. A number of allowances and deductions can reduce the tax bill. These are mainly personal and general allowances which are related to age, dependants, disability, pension payments, mortgage repayments and charitable donations. Medical fees, medical insurance and school fees are not deductible.

A resident with one property as a main residence and another rented out will pay the same type of taxes as the non resident. The income tax rates will be more sympathetic but the other property taxes will remain the same. A resident should simply add the rental income to other income when making an annual Spanish income tax declaration.

Capital gains tax

Liability to capital gains applies to residents and non residents. Capital gains are payable on the profit from the sale of assets in Spain such as property, stocks and shares, antiques, art and jewellery. Since most ex-pats will have arranged their investments free of tax, capital gains in practice should only apply to property. A capital gain is based on the difference between the purchase price and the selling price of the property, less the costs of buying and selling and the cost of any improvement.

For residents, if the property is owned for less than two years the gain is added to income and taxed accordingly. If the property is owned for more than two years the gain is reduced by an inflation coefficient. Tax is payable at the individual's income tax rate with a fixed deduction before payment. For those over 65 years of age the gain is tax-free.

For non residents the gain is taxed at a flat 35%. The two-year ownership rule and inflation factor allowance still applies – age exemption does not.

Wealth tax

Spanish residents should be able to avoid this tax as it is for the very wealthy. They are required to pay wealth tax on their worldwide assets less any liabilities. The assets are defined as property, vehicles, jewellery and investments and cash in hand at the bank. Liabilities include mortgages and other debts. The first 110,000 Euros are free of tax (double that for a couple) and thereafter taxed on a sliding scale commencing at 0.2%.

For non residents again harsher penalties accrue. They pay wealth tax at the same rate as residents on their Spanish assets but have no tax-free allowance. If they are wise however, they will have no assets registered in Spain, while the tax on a property asset will have been included in *Patrimonio* tax.

Inheritance tax

Inheritance tax is certainly the most complicated of all taxes and needs specialised advice to legitimately reduce any liability upon death.

◆ Inheritance tax is payable if the recipient is a resident of Spain or the assets being passed on death are property in Spain.

◆ Inheritance tax is paid by the beneficiaries and not by the deceased's estate.

◆ Inheritance tax starts on a sliding scale after a fixed allowance of 16,000 Euros per recipient.

◆ The cornerstone of avoiding inheritance tax is to have a Spanish will for Spanish assets, good financial advice and the possible use of an inheritance trust.

There is no exemption between husband and wife for the joint ownership of a property. In many countries a property can be held in joint names. If one person dies the property passes automatically to the other person. This is not the case in Spain where each person holds an equal share, which upon the death of one person is subject to inheritance tax and succession law.

The value of a property can be reduced by 95% for the purposes of inheritance tax when the principal residence is bequeathed to a spouse, parent or child who has been living with the deceased for two years prior to death and when the inheritors own the property ten years from the date of death.

Yet another method of reducing inheritance tax is the peculiarly Spanish method of setting up a *usufructo* (a life interest). In this situation the ownership of the house can pass to the children leaving the life interest holders free to live in the property for the rest of their lifetime. Legitimate this may be, easy to set up, but perhaps more suited to passing down the family home from generation to generation.

IS IT BETTER TO FORM A COMPANY?

A buy-to-let investor with more than one letting property in Spain would do well to consider the benefits of forming a company. Make sure the company is legally registered and is paying all the correct taxes for being engaged in a multi-site activity or providing hotel-type services. This moves the investor into a new legal area. It is now a business, which opens the door to IVA (value added tax) and more importantly the deduction of expenses, such as maintenance and depreciation. Put another way, taxes are paid on the profit made rather than on the income of the individual.

What type of company?

An EU national or a permanent resident with an NIE and *residencia* can be self-employed (*trabajador autónomo*) or work as a sole trader (*empresa individual*).

A self-employed person does not have the protection of a limited company should the business fail. It may be advantageous to operate as a limited company, but 'limited companies' cannot be purchased off the shelf. A *gestor* can do this, but it usually takes some time.

A business may assume various legal titles. Most small businessmen and women operate as sole traders and register with the appropriate trade association, pay a small entrance fee and a monthly subscription. A small company is usually a private limited company (*Sociedad de responsabilidad Limitada*) designated SL. It is the simplest and most common form of limited company and does not have any public shares. A large limited company is a public company (*Sociedad Anonima*) designated SA, which is similar to an American Inc or a British Plc. To form an SA requires a minimum of share capital, at least 50 employees and one director.

Social security

All self-employed people and businesses must register with the social security scheme. The cost of social security contributions for the self-employed is higher than for employees and the benefits less.

Impuesto sobre Actividades Economicas (IAE)

All self-employed people and businesses pay to the local Town Hall (*ayuntamiento*) tax known as IAE. What is it? They say it is a tax on economic activities. It may be, but it is similar to a local tax payment on a private house and is collected in the same way. The cost of IAE varies considerably depending on the profession or business, where it is located, the number employed and the size the premises.

Impuesto sobre el Valor Anadido (IVA)

All self-employed people and businesses must register for value added tax (IVA) and levy this tax on all services or goods.

OWNING PROPERTY BY A CORPORATE OR TRUST STRUCTURE

For a property speculator with many rented properties the advantage of using a corporate holding structure, or an offshore holding trust, must be examined. Trusts in particular are an important tool in tax planning.

Spanish inheritance tax is avoided. Inheritance tax is payable on the death of the owner of a Spanish property irrespective of the tax residency of the owner. As a company never dies, a Spanish property owned by a company will not be subject to any inheritance tax in Spain.

Spanish capital gains tax is avoided. This tax is payable on the gain in value of the property when resold. The tax is payable irrespective of the tax residency of the owner. Liability to this tax can be avoided as, by transferring the shares in the company, disposal of the property does not take place.

Elimination of IVA and notary fees. A corporate structure avoids a prospective purchaser having to pay these taxes. IVA can also be avoided on new buildings if the construction takes place within the company.

SUMMARY

◆ For a non resident, rental income is taxed at 25%.

◆ For a resident the rental income is added to other income and taxed accordingly.

- ◆ For a buy-to-let investor with two or more properties the benefits of forming a company must be considered.

- ◆ With many properties in a portfolio a corporate structure or a trust should be considered.

Having Fun

A buy-to-let is for profit ... and fun. How? By enjoying the healthy food, drinking the excellent wine, going outdoors into the countryside, taking part in some sporting activities, joining social activities and learning about the culture and customs of the country.

ENJOYING THE FOOD

Although the Mediterranean diet is healthy, the hour it is eaten is not. The Spanish are famous for eating at a time which to some is ludicrously late in the day. Who in most countries would think of sitting down to a full meal at nine or ten o'clock in the evening? This late night eating is all to do with the Spanish siesta-adjusted body clock with most people not finishing work until half past seven or eight o'clock.

Restaurant meals usually consist of three courses. The choices for *Menu del Dia* are chalked up on a blackboard outside the restaurant. Many restaurants in Spain (including, strangely, Chinese) offer a *Menu del Dia*. It must consist of three courses plus bread and water or wine. The third course is always dessert. The price is always less than if you were to order the same items *à la carte*. It is one of the best deals in Spain. There may be only two or three choices per course or as many as a dozen.

With a bottle of table wine and food at prices that do not compare with those paid for a meal in northern Europe, eating out can cost next to nothing. It is a constant source of amazement that restaurants can produce a three course meal with wine for as little as 10 Euros. A service charge is included in some restaurant and hotel bills, but waiters appreciate an addition 5–10% tip.

But beware! Among the basic intake of food and drink should be included tobacco. Men smoke, women smoke and teenagers smoke. Wherever you go you will soon be enveloped in a thick blue haze of cigarette smoke and many Spaniards seem not to have the faintest idea that this could be uncomfortable to anyone.

In addition to restaurants, there are many attractive *tapas* bars offering freshly made snacks and appetisers. The *tapas* bar is unique to Spain. Alicante is known as one of the best *tapas* areas where the ritual of *tapas* eating has reached sublime levels.

Tapas come in all sorts of delicious forms and are readily available in most bars. Rows of dishes are arranged in a chilled cabinet in front of the customer. They comprise tortilla, spicy meat balls, big plump olives, sausages, fried aubergines, egg salad, courgettes, spicy potatoes, liver, cheese, serrano ham, sardines, prawns in garlic, anchovies, mussels, *calamares* (fried squid), *sepia* (cuttlefish) and small fish in olive oil.

Nibbling at small amounts of food is popular, but of equal importance is that the *tapas* bar is an essential part of life, a place where people meet to eat and drink, to gossip, to carry out business and generally pass the time of day.

THE MEDITERRANEAN DIET

When the death rates from coronary heart disease in different countries are compared to the levels of fat intake, there is a strong tendency for the rates to be highest in the countries where people eat the most fat. At the head of the list are the Finns, who eat a lot of meat and cheese, and at the bottom are the Japanese, who eat very little. Americans come near the top, but the most striking deviation from this trend are the French, who have the same fat intake as Americans, but only one quarter the death rate from heart disease.

The Greeks too break all the rules, and yet their risk of heart disease is low. The life expectancy of a 45-year-old Greek man is about two years longer than for an Englishman or American of the same age. Greek men smoke heavily, drink alcohol regularly, rarely indulge in recreational exercise, and eat a high-salt, high-fat diet.

Figure 13. Mediterranean food pyramid.

What is the answer to this paradox? The only rational explanation is the nature of the diet. The critical factor appears to be not how much fat is eaten, but what sort. What distinguishes the diets of Spaniards and other Mediterranean peoples is that they get their fat as monounsaturated fat because their cuisine is based on olive oil. Other features of the Mediterranean diet are a high intake of fruits and vegetables, and relatively low meat consumption. Complex carbohydrates are a major component, in the form of wholegrain breads, grains and cereals. The lesson to be learned is that you do not have to go on a low-fat diet to cut your risk of heart disease; what you need to do is make sure that the fat you eat is mostly monounsaturated.

The basis of the traditional Mediterranean diet is a three level pyramid where the foods at the top should be consumed less frequently than the ones at the bottom (see Figure 13).

The sole occupant of the apex of the pyramid is red meat. A lot of evidence now suggests that a high meat intake is associated not only with heart disease but also with colon and prostate cancers. Furthermore, all the nutrients found in meat can be obtained from other sources.

In the middle are sweets. Desserts (other than fruit) are not a part of the Mediterranean diet. Next are eggs, which are restricted because of their cholesterol content. Poultry, which is a preferable source of protein to red meat, follows, but it is not as good as fish, which comes at the bottom of this group, and should be eaten several times per week.

At the bottom of the pyramid come dairy products (principally cheese and yogurt), which can be taken daily, but in small amounts. This does not mean drinking a lot of whole milk (drinking milk is not a feature of the Mediterranean diet), and low-fat cheeses may be prefer-able. Next comes olive oil, which is used instead of butter, margarine, and other cooking oils. Followed by fruits, beans, nuts (good sources of protein) and vegetables. Finally there are breads, pasta, rice, other grains and potatoes.

DRINKING THE WINE

The Spanish are casual in their attitude to wine. They do not take it seriously, drinking mostly young table wines. At the same price as a bottle of water, a carton of milk, or a soft drink it is something that can be taken or left with a meal. In a restaurant frequented by working men having their lunch, half a bottle of unwanted red wine is frequently discarded. Wine is cheaper in Spain than in many other countries. A good quality rioja only costs 3 Euros and it has not increased greatly over the years.

Spain has a long history of wine production, with old stone wine presses still evident in the mountains. Storage in oak casts followed in the 15th century. In the 1960s Miguel Torres established the first stainless steel wine-making equipment in his Catalan winery giving precise control over the fermentation procedures. Most producers followed suit and now Barcelona is a world centre for the manufacture of wine-making equipment. This forward-looking attitude has given rise to a new approach to Spanish wine-making. After almost 2,500 years we can now enjoy the best of Spanish wines: nutty, dry and light, oaky reds with cinnamon depth, clean crisp whites, herby reds and new sparkling wines.

The extraordinary diversity of wines produced in Spain is due not only to the skill of the winemaker but also to the country's different climatic and soil conditions. There are three main soil types: chalk, a bedrock called schist and clay. Chalk and schist provide water retention during the driest part of the year while clay is rich in trace elements such as iron.

There is a downside to Spanish wine. A lot of mediocre 'plonk' is still produced and if suffers from a poor international reputation. This has much to do with marketing, as the quality of Spanish wine has improved enormously over the last few decades with the introduction of new grape varieties and more consistency in processing.

Drinking red wine is good, hence the old Spanish proverb 'wine was made for kings, and water for donkeys'. Red wine is well known to have valuable health benefits which are said to range from helping fight heart disease and cancer to warding off Alzheimer's and increasing life expectancy. There is even some evidence that, in contrast to other alcoholic beverages, it does not suppress the immune system. As well as being an enjoyable and affordable part of the Mediterranean diet, wine provides antioxidants as well as many other health benefits. Red wine as part of a daily diet keeps the body healthy.

The wine we drink alters the levels of lipids (fats) in blood. It lowers the total cholesterol count, and raises the high-density lipoprotein (HDL) or 'good cholesterol' levels. In layman's terms, it keeps the blood vessels clean. Wine can help fight cancer as it contains the cancer suppressant resvatrol. The red grapes that go into red wine also have bioflavonoids, which are antioxidants and help prevent cancer. Wine helps fight stress and relaxes cancer patients thus helping them fight their disease.

Studies have also shown that red wine can help prevent heart strokes. The relaxing influence of a glass of wine can help the body to unwind after a stressful day at work. Researchers have found that those who drink up to three glasses a day regularly are healthier than non wine drinkers and than those who drink more than this amount.

Drinking wine, like anything else done excessively, can harm your body. The key to enjoying the benefits is moderation. Red wine is also a triggering factor for migraine headaches as it contains high levels of tannins. However, the benefits for most people far outweigh the drawbacks. Remember that hangovers are not really from the alcohol – they are from the impurities in the wine; so choose good quality wine thus avoiding the ex-pats proverb, 'Red sky in the morning, red wine the previous evening'.

LIFE OUTDOORS

Spain is an outdoor country. Sunshine simply means that a minimum of time is spent indoors. The only real way to learn about the country is to travel. While there are other methods, such as reading books and tourist guides or watching travel films, it is only by going to see a place that the true ambience can be obtained. There are places where you can enjoy the sun, the sea and the mountains. Places where you can benefit from the climate and keep in shape with a favourite all year round sport. Places where you can discover local history and monuments, travel down hidden byways and forest tracks, participate in local fiestas, meet local people ... and much more.

The diverse geographical nature of Spain, with its mountains, woodlands, beaches and sea gives a wonderful backdrop for sporting activities. Golf clubs, sports centres, bowling greens, gymnasiums, swimming pools, marinas and tennis clubs promote better use of leisure time.

The principal sporting activity in Spain, which of course often impacts on the location of a property, is golf. The lush green fairways, often set in a barren landscape, are an oasis for a property with a view and a mecca for golfers seeking to escape the winters of northern Europe.

In Scotland, the home of golf, it is a game for the working man. In Spain it is a game for the tourist and the wealthy resident. The boom in Spain is in direct contrast to golf in the UK where they are feeling the pinch. Memberships are falling, joining fees are down by 42% and the number of rounds on municipal courses has fallen by 26%. Private clubs are rethinking their position and price.

Another principal leisure activity is hiking. Walking or hiking clubs exist in all the main areas. For the adventurous the best places to go are the Picos de Europe in northern Spain, the Pyrenees near the French border, the Costa Blanca inland from Benidorm and around the Sierra Nevada near Granada. Many holiday companies offer Spanish walking tours. This has given rise to some excellent English language publications describing good detailed routes with clear concise maps. The trails themselves are well marked and the only hazards are dogs and the unhygienic nature of some refuge huts. It is important not to underestimate some of these rugged trails with rapidly changing weather, snow on high ground and exposure on steep paths.

Other sporting activities enjoyed in Spain are:

- bowling
- sailing
- fishing
- tennis
- running
- gymnasiums
- beach sports
- skiing.

Figure 14. Spain's outdoor activities.

MIXING SOCIALLY

Foreigners seek their own wherever they go, but perhaps the English-speaking with more enthusiasm than other nationalities. Some pursue intensely social lives within the community while some deliberately shun the company of their compatriots.

Figure 15. Spain's more leisurely activities.

In the early stages of visiting Spain the support received from other expatriates is often important in cementing friendships and forming social networks. The newcomer is typically ascribed a subordinate or dependent role, seniority among expatriates being mainly determined by their length of residence. A second influence is the degree of permanence versus seasonality of residence, as long-term residents tend to look down on tourists, even those of their own nationality.

In 1992 the BBC filmed an ill-fated soap drama near Mijas, creating an image that the British expatriate community in the Costa del Sol lived in an artificial world. The programme based on a conceived stereotype of 'Brits in Spain' presented them as living an idle existence in the sun, drinking too much alcohol, behaving like old colonials, and certainly not integrating into the Spanish way of life. Sometimes the ex-pats were portrayed as having a wonderful time, on other occasions as being poor and isolated, while the presence of a few exiled criminals was turned into all manner of stories.

Of course it is not true! While elderly British residents rarely integrate effectively with local Spaniards, they enjoy a well-structured lifestyle which on the whole keeps them busy, happy and healthy. They also join the many expatriate clubs, which cater for a wide range of activities and interests. Many people join these clubs to meet people of similar background and interests and to widen social circles. Social clubs are a method of meeting people, of sharing a common interest, past or present. They are meeting places to deal with problems or to seek information. They are an aid to settling in a new country. Golf and hiking may be the top sports but a meal, a drink or a visit to the club, are the main social activities.

Another sign of social activity is the proliferation of English-language media. English, Scottish and Irish newspapers are available on the morning of publication, and there are several locally produced papers and magazines. English-speaking digital TV and FM radio stations confirm the view that very few Britons read Spanish newspapers or watch Spanish television – apart from the weather forecast.

LEARNING THE A – Z OF CUSTOMS AND CULTURE

Ayuntamiento
To the ordinary Spaniard life starts and stops at the *Ayuntamiento* (the Town Hall). Situated in the *plaza*

mayor of each village, town or city the building is bedecked with flags of the *comunidad*, the country and Europe, signifying its importance as the focus of everyday life. The Town Hall is the home of the *Municipio*, a council headed by a mayor and a number of councillors all of whom are elected. It is responsible for keeping the streets clean, collecting garbage, street lighting, water supply and sewerage, roads, cemeteries, schools, planning, traffic control, parks, libraries, markets, social services, fire prevention and public sports facilities. It is at the Town Hall where some taxes are paid, where licences are issued, where the right to vote is granted and where births and deaths are recorded.

Bullfighting

This is not the place to discuss the morality of a bullfight but it is worth making one important point. Most foreigners are aware that in the bullfight several bulls are going to be injured in various ways. They will be lanced, they will have sharp barbs stuck in them and in the end they will be killed, more or less efficiently, with a sword. There will be blood and there will be death. If a foreigner does not want to see this, or may be upset by it, or if they think it is barbaric and cruel, then it is really not worth going because they will certainly not enjoy it.

Bull running

The world-famous event involving fighting bulls is of course the Pamplona Bull Run. There are many other fiestas in Spanish towns and villages where young and frisky, lean and mean fighting bulls are turned loose in closed-off roads and squares. Bulls are not injured in these events but the only real defence against them are good strong legs. It is important to stress that there is nothing fake about these events. The bulls are real and extremely dangerous and people, even experienced runners, have been badly injured or killed. If you enjoy raw excitement and the thrill of adrenalin pumping through your system then you will certainly find it running the bulls.

Conversation

One important characteristic to be relied upon is the Spaniards' readiness to communicate. Compare the discreet silence of a group of English people who do not know each other to the friendly chatter which quickly develops among a similar group of Spanish people. A good deal of social life is maintained *en la calle* (in the street) or any public place. Bars are particularly important. Spaniards generally enjoy conversation, invariably loud, where everyone seems to talk at once in an excited babble of noise.

Crime

Spain does have a high petty crime rate. Homes have to be protected by security grilles on doors and windows. Cash, passports and electrical goods are the main targets. The theft of motor scooters is so high that insurance companies do not accept this risk. The police seem unable to reduce these incidents, necessitating citizens to ensure protection of their own person and property. Pickpockets, operating in gangs, are active at all open-air markets, indoor markets and within some supermarkets, particularly when thronged with people during the busy summer season. It is wrong to point the finger at any nationality, or social or occupational group because this is the result of increased prosperity within a tolerant society. While murder, bank robbery and crimes of passion are reported in the popular press, these are a rarity. As long as sensible precautions are taken, the streets of Spain are safe for both adults and children.

ETA

Internally Spain is still troubled by the Basque separatist group called ETA. Now officially classed as a terrorist organisation there seems to be the political will in Madrid to deal with this problem that has resulted in a significant number of murders each year. Since 1968 over 800 people have been killed by ETA – mostly high profile public citizens.

Family group

The family group is strong with sometimes two or three generations living within one house. The Spanish love of children is well known. Children will be beautifully dressed with a confidence that befits offspring in the new millennium. Mother and father will be proud parents with a deep sense of honour. Grandparents will be friendly, courteous, generous, not fully comprehending the staggering changes that have taken place since their childhood. Young Spaniards are the same as the young of any European country, seeking freedom, equality and enjoyment alongside their worldly brothers and sisters.

Fiestas

Fiestas celebrate a national religious occasion or local thanksgiving where towns and cities come to a stop as men, women and children dress up to enjoy themselves aided by a plentiful supply of food, wine and laughter. Processions with music start the evening, dancing and singing follow. Fireworks close the evening with a loud colourful bang. Each fiesta has its own distinctive character – sounds, colours, flavours, smells, costumes, rituals and a typical dish. There are celebrations for the dead and the living. Some fiestas appease the forces of nature. Others drive out evil spirits. Often they are religious historical events or medieval customs. There is always a fiesta somewhere. They can last for a day, a week or a fortnight.

Flamenco

The popular romantic image of Spain, namely flamenco, singing and dancing gypsies and swaggering bullfighters is unreal. But flamenco does occupy an important place in Spanish culture, particularly in Andalucian culture. It is not simply preserved folklore, but rather a vibrant and important art of song and dance accompanied by mesmeric hand clapping. It is certainly true that a version of flamenco has been commercialised and turned into a sanitised spectacle. This sometimes bears little relation to the raw vigour of the real thing.

Gambling and the lottery

Like the people of all the Mediterranean countries, the Spaniard loves to gamble. It is however focused on the state national lottery (*Loteria Nacional*) run in aid of charities, for which tickets can be purchased at offices, from street vendors and through the Society for the Blind (ONCE). The world's biggest lottery takes place each Christmas (*El Gordo*). Ticket prices are high and therefore mainly sold to syndicates with the winners arguing over the spoils. *El Nino* (The Kid), the second biggest lottery, takes place in early January.

Getting things done

Although the country has transformed itself into a tolerant, democratic society it is still trying to shake off the shackles of the era when heavyweight bureaucracy ruled the day. Great strides have been made but there is still a long way to go as the decentralised government battles with duplication of effort and unnecessary bureaucracy. Red tape stifles simple daily transactions and frustrates all nationalities including Spaniards themselves. Spanish bureaucrats, in common with those of other nations, when asked to render a service often find it easier to say 'no' than to say 'yes'.

Spaniards are, in general, insistent in their demands, whether this be in a market, bar or government office. They most certainly do not easily accept 'no' for an answer and new residents should not either. When something really needs to be done, which is being refused, it is best to remain patient but persistent. Losing your temper or becoming angry in such circumstances is counter-productive. The trick is to maintain a conversation, keep the bureaucrat's attention and get them to respond to you as a person and not simply a problem. So much in Spain is achieved through a network of individual contacts and friends of friends that many problems can be resolved through these channels. It is not always possible to buy your way out of problems or difficulties, but things do get done for friends.

Language

Castellano Spanish is the romance language of the country. *Catalan*, modified French, is spoken in the north east. Valenciano, Basque and Galician are other difficult to understand regional dialects. 200 million people speak Spanish worldwide, mainly in the former Spanish Empire, making it the third most popular language after English and Chinese. English is the business language in Madrid and Barcelona. It is well understood on the Costas and Islands, but is rarely spoken or understood in rural areas.

Language barrier

A foreigner, away from the areas of mass tourism, may well be stared at as an object of curiosity, but it is easy to turn this around and attempt to overcome the language barrier by starting a simple conversation with odd phrases and expressive gestures. Spaniards are generally pleased when a foreigner makes an effort to speak their language. They are remarkably patient with someone who is trying to communicate and they listen carefully in an attempt to make sense of the mangled grammar and odd vocabulary. Exactly 'how' it is said it is less important than 'wanting' to say it.

Mañana

One major downside of Spain is its cultural feature called *mañana* – never do something today if it can be put off to tomorrow, or the day after, or perhaps never to be done at all. To live successfully in Spain it is necessary to come to terms with its culture. Coping with *mañana* is a necessary skill that just has to be acquired. It is best seen with builders, repairmen, when a car breaks down or indeed any occurrence requiring a commitment to a time or date. A shrug of the shoulders, an upturned hand, a slight bow of the head, a moment of silence is *mañana* in progress. Do not fight it, as no single person can change the culture of a nation. No matter how difficult, learn to live with it. *Mañana* does not apply to services such as trains, buses or planes. It is also said that the only thing that starts on time in Spain is a bullfight.

Monarchy

The King of Spain is Juan Carlos I. The Royal Family have a palace in Madrid and another in Mallorca. The Spanish monarchy was restored in 1975. Although Franco nominated Juan Carlos as his heir this blessing was initially regarded as being a tarred brush. However, he energetically supported the transition to democracy. The long simmering resentment in military circles against rapid change resulted in an attempted coup to seize power in 1981. King Carlos narrowly foiled the coup by convincing most of the military units to remain loyal to the Government. His courageous opposition to the attempted coup made him a hero.

Moors and Christians

No one loves a good procession as much as the Spanish. The Moors and Christians fiestas are fun, they offer a great spectacle affording a glimpse through the darkened glass of history at another Spain, a Spain forged on an anvil of blood and fire, a Spain that easily slips back through the centuries to the glory days of battle and blood, of victory or defeat, of fire and warfare.

The whole festival celebrates the liberation of Spain from Moorish domination, finalised in 1492 and ironically a collapse of the great Iberian civilization into religious intolerance. The wailing of the horns, the rhythmic beat of the marching drums and, above all, the awesome crash of the gigantic wheel-borne kettle drums boom out their song of blood and destruction. The mock battles end with a victory for the Christians, and utter defeat for the Moors.

It is a strange celebration, for the Moors made a massive contribution to Spain and in retrospect the Christians led the country into utter decay. But such deep reflections are for later, not during the awesome spectacle of a well-staged Moors and Christians fiesta.

Equally strange, the participants seem to take far more time and trouble to produce costumes of dazzling complexity for the Moors, whilst the Christians wear the inevitable bland cross-bedecked tabard, with a variety of exotic helmets. Making the costumes is big business, with whole factories devoted to this never-to-be-forgotten industry.

Nightclubs

Along busy main roads or in cities, flashing neon lights beckon the unwary into a nightclub. These are not cabaret, musical or dancing extravaganzas. If not eating, drinking red wine or singing, the Spanish male has a reputation of being a great lover. That may or may not be the case, and for all we know a nightclub may be the place to learn, for they are often registered or unregistered brothels.

Paseo

Outside the restaurant, in the main square or along the promenade the evening *paseo* will commence with young girls and boys, parents and grandparents strolling in a leisurely manner. For some it is gentle exercise in the cool of the evening, for others a prelude to a good night out. For the spectators, it is an entertainment. In villages chairs are placed in the narrow streets, oblivious to passing traffic, as occupants emerge from their houses to talk and gossip about the days events.

Politeness

Anyone who has spent a short time in Spain will know that its people are friendly. If you are polite, smile and offer locals a greeting in their own language it will go a long way to establishing and maintaining relationships. However it would be fair to say that, in tourist resorts a perceived need to extract the maximum Euros in the minimum time has eroded some of the natural charm of the Spaniard. A few Spaniards too find it difficult to handle their new found wealth. But it would be wrong to categorise the whole country by the behaviour patterns of a few. As one might expect, there is a contrast between the older and younger generations. The more elderly Spaniard will have endured the repression of the Franco years, may be illiterate and have worked in agriculture. In contrast his offspring will be vibrant, computer literate, with a city-based mentality that embraces new cosmopolitan values.

Pride

Familiarity is a hallmark of Spanish life. Handshaking and kissing on the cheek is the usual form of greeting.

Old-fashioned courtliness and formal manners are, however, still a custom in rural areas. Great store is set by personal loyalty and friendship, but it is also very important to take account of a Spaniard's personal sense of honour and pride, which is easily offended.

Religion

Catholicism is still an influence over Spanish society. Although church attendance is falling, on a Sunday around midday families can be seen dressed in their best attire strolling home from their place of worship. The images of saints watch over shops, bars and drivers' cabs. Traditional fiestas mark church feasts. However, during the Civil War the Church aligned itself with Franco and some people have never forgiven it for this.

Siesta

A change in working hours to match northern Europe is reducing the importance of the siesta. But in some parts of Spain it is still a common practice and it is best to expect very little activity between 1.30 p.m. and about 4.30 p.m., when offices, public buildings and shops tend to be closed. The siesta is, however, particularly significant during the summer when many parts of Spain are blisteringly hot and the only sensible thing to do is to rest behind closed shutters. A siesta also allows the body to deal with late Spanish nightlife.

Toilets

Try to find a public toilet in Spain – it's easier to find a needle in a haystack. Except in railway stations, shopping centres and places of public interest they don't exist. What do you do? Answer, go to a bar, cafe, hotel or restaurant nearby. Owners of food establishments are well accustomed to this behaviour, granting a request to use their facilities with a smile or a wave of the hand.

SUMMARY

♦ The Mediterranean diet is healthy but beware of eating at ridiculously late hours.

♦ The red wine too is good for you but only in moderation.

♦ Spain is an outdoor country. Travel it. Enjoy the facilities on offer.

♦ *Eldorado* is a myth. English-speaking people integrate into Spanish life to a limited degree as they do seek their own.

♦ Fiestas, flamenco and bullfighting may be the traditional image of Spain but that disguises a dynamic, modern country, confident with its place in Europe.

(13)

Past, Present and Future

LOOKING BACK

In order to run a successful business an eye should be kept on cash flow, occupancy rates, payments and how things are going according to plan for the current and projected periods. It is best to sit down regularly and formally review the situation, attending to any problems that need fixing. Although every business suffers setbacks it is important to be realistic, to act promptly, to deal with issues and not ignore them. Should the issues be financial there are only three ways to proceed – increase revenue, cut costs or both. Should the issue be cash flow there is only one way to proceed – get the money in quicker.

WHERE WE ARE

When a business has reached a successful plateau after a number of years some questions have to be asked. Do you continue running it? Are you happy with it? What do you wish to do next? Do you wish to expand? If so, in what direction? Success can breed success, with the initial terrors of being a landlord and investing huge sums of money to induce paying tenants soon forgotten.

The expansionist option can always makes sense as it reduces overhead costs – advertising two properties costs no more than advertising one. There are constant offers of loans from banks and other financial institutions, which many people believe to be a modern way to riches through credit. They may be right, provided it is possible to sleep easy at night knowing vast sums of money are owed to a lender. When interest rates are low it is possible to acquire many properties extremely quickly.

Investing in property can become addictive. No sooner is one Spanish apartment up and running successfully, than another one can be considered. Looking every week through property magazines and the property sections of newspapers are addictive signs. Clicking away, calculating yields, is yet another.

The next step is obvious – become a proud owner of an identical property close to the first one. Little risk in that! Perhaps buy a third. By now one is well on the way to becoming a portfolio landlord, regarding it as a business rather than a lucrative sideline but still enjoying the experience, getting a buzz out of it, making sure the books balance and the yields are satisfactory, taking a risk Spanish property inflation will still be one of the highest in the world, and who knows ...

MOVING AHEAD

Owning rental property does not have to be hard work. It is a serious business, but there's no reason why it has to be a routine job. To do it correctly should not take more than a few days a month, no matter how many properties are owned. To become a multiple landlord there are four simple principles:

- Buy the correct property in the correct location.

- Market the property correctly.

- Attract the right tenants at the right price.

- Do not manage the property – manage the people – tour operators, agents, tenants and your own time.

Moving ahead is not just limited to more properties. It may mean moving up to a hostel or a hotel, which in rural tourist areas is aided by a government grant. It can mean becoming a letting agent or a holiday company. All are expansionist opportunities in Spain.

SUMMARY

- Becoming a serial landlord does make sense. Building on a solid base, using the plentiful supply of money, reducing overhead costs and managing people are keys to even greater success.

- Other opportunities exist – particularly in rural areas aided by government grants.

Appendix 1

Demographics and Politics at a Glance

Statistics

Population:	40.3 million
Population growth:	0.5% (average 1997–2001)
Land area:	504,782 square kilometres
Currency:	Euro
GDP:	Euro 650.2 billion
GDP growth:	3.9% (average 1997–2001)
Inflation:	2.6% (average 1997–2001)
Unemployment:	13.05%
Labour cost per hour:	10.94 Euros

Geography

Mainland Spain covers an area of half a million square kilometres and has a coastline of 2,100 kilometres. Spain includes both the Canary and Balearic Islands, administers two small enclaves in Morocco known as Ceuta and Melilla and three island groups near Africa. The British dependency of Gibraltar is situated at Spain's southern extremity.

It is a big country, the second largest in Europe after France. The interior of Spain is a vast plateau called the Meseta bound to the north east by the Pyrenees, in the south west by the Sierra Morena and in the south by the best known Sierra Nevada. The Meseta makes Spain the highest, most mountainous area of Europe. Across the Meseta itself many rivers have cut deep valleys. Much of the coastline is steep and rocky but there is a narrow coastal plain bordering the Mediterranean. The highest point is Pico de Tiede on Tenerife at 3,718 metres above sea level.

Population

The population of 40 million is less than many European countries. Spain, despite being 97% a Catholic country, has a low birth rate and a high life expectancy of 75 years for men and 80 years for women. Many Spaniards are now urban dwellers. Madrid, the capital, has the largest conurbation. Approaching one million British live in Spain concentrated in Madrid, Barcelona, the Costas and the Islands.

Political structure

Following the death of General Franco in 1975, Spain embarked on a political transition to democracy. After the legalisation of political parties, the first free election for 40 years was held in 1977. In 1978 a referendum approved a new democratic constitution and repealed many of the laws of the Franco era. The parliament, or *Cortes*, is bicameral; real power resides in the 350-seat lower house (Congress of Deputies); the upper house (Senate) has 208 directly elected members and 51 regional representatives. Parliament is elected for a maximum four year term, but early dissolution is possible. Decentralisation, which has devolved a considerable degree of power to the 17 regions or autonomous communities, is a characteristic of the Constitution. In 1986 Spain joined the EU. It currently accounts for 12% of the EU's population and 8% of its output. All the main political parties are firmly committed to playing an active role within the EU.

Policy issues

By securing Spain's participation in the EU's single currency, the Popular Party government achieved one of the primary objectives that it set itself on entering office. The major economic policy challenge facing the government is to maintain an appropriate balance between national fiscal policy and monetary policy in the Euro area, and to ensure that unemployment continues to fall without stimulating inflation. The government will also have to decide whether constitutional reform, to which it is opposed, is a price worth paying for delivering a long-term solution to the troubled Basque Country.

Exports	% of total
Raw materials and intermediate goods	44.4
Consumer goods	40.5
Capital goods	12.1
Energy	2.9

Imports	% of total
Raw materials and intermediate goods	45.5
Consumer goods	26.3
Capital goods	16.8
Energy	11.3

Leading markets	% of total
France	19.5
Germany	11.8
Portugal	10.0
Italy	9.0
EU	71.3

Leading suppliers	% of total
France	16.8
Germany	15.5
Italy	9.1
UK	7.0
EU	63.9

Appendix 2

Knowing Your Way Around

Airports

Alicante	Tel: 966919000	Fax: 966919354
Barcelona	Tel: 932983838	Fax: 932983737
Bilbao	Tel: 944869300	Fax: 944869313
Ibiza	Tel: 971809000	Fax: 971809287
Jerez	Tel: 956150000	Fax: 956150061
Lanzarote	Tel: 928846001	Fax: 928846022
Las Palmas	Tel: 928579000	Fax: 928579117
Madrid	Tel: 913058343	Fax: 913936200
Malaga	Tel: 952048844	Fax: 952048777
Palma de Mallorca	Tel: 971789099	Fax: 971789010
Santiago de Compostela	Tel: 981547501	Fax: 981547507
Sevilla	Tel: 954449011	Fax: 954449025
Tenerife South	Tel: 922759000	Fax: 922759247
Valencia	Tel: 961598515	Fax: 961598510

Babies

Baby foods and disposable nappies are available in all resorts and are obtainable from supermarkets and chemists.

Banking hours

Most banks open from 8.30 a.m.–2.00 p.m. Monday to Friday and 8.30 a.m. to 1.00 p.m. on Saturdays (except in the summer).

Church services

Information on the location of churches and timetables of religious services should be sought locally.

Consular assistance

British Consulates in Spain will assist holidaymakers in emergencies. They can provide a list of local lawyers, interpreters and doctors. They can also give guidance in tracing missing persons. (See Appendix 10.)

Credit Cards

Most hotels, garages and department stores accept major credit cards, but this should be checked before each transaction. Some additional identification may be required.

Currency

From 1 January 2002, the Euro (€) became the currency of Spain. There are five denominations of notes – 5, 10, 20, 50, and 500 Euros, and eight different coins – 1 and 2 Euros and 1, 2, 5, 10, 20 and 50 cents. 1 Euro equals 166 old Pesetas. The import or export of cash, notes and bearer-cheques, in any currency, including Euros, is subject to declaration where the amount exceeds 6,000 Euro per person per journey. The export from Spain of cash, notes and bearer-cheques, in any currency, including Euros, is subject to declaration where the amount exceeds 30,000 Euros per person and journey.

Duty free

Allowances on imports from EU countries no longer exist but are still applicable to goods purchased outside the EU. Limits on imports of duty paid goods bought in the

EU into the UK are generous, provided they are for personal consumption. For full details contact Customs and Excise on Tel: 020 7202 4227 or www.hmce.gov.uk.

Electricity
Voltage 220 or 225 AC. Plugs are two pin.

Entry requirements
A full British passport, valid for the duration of the visit, is required to enter mainland Spain, the Balearic and Canary Islands. EU citizens do not require visas for visits of up to 90 days. For stays over 90 days residence permits are required.

Health service
British tourists visiting Spain, covered by the National Insurance scheme, will enjoy free medical assistance under the Spanish Health Service during their stay. Please contact the local Health Authority Office for further assistance. Form E111 is available from the Post Office. Long-term residents, over normal retiring age, are entitled to join the Spanish health system. Form E121 from the Social Security Services in Newcastle is required.

Insurance
Holidaymakers are advised to take out adequate holiday insurance. This is available from most tour operators and travel agents.

Mail
Post correspondence from Spain with Spanish Post Office stamps in official post boxes or at hotels displaying the logo *Correos y Telegrafos*.

Maps

Walking maps may be obtained from Servicio de Publicaciones del Instituto Geográfico Nacional, General lbanez de Ibero, 28003 Madrid. Tel: (0034) 915979684 Fax: (0034) 915352591. Large scale maps can be obtained from specialist book dealers Stanfords Ltd., 12–14 Long Acre, Covent Garden, London WC2E 9LP. Tel: 020 7836 1321 Fax: 020 7836 0189.

Metal detectors

Metal detecting is a strictly controlled activity in Spain and its practice in public places requires a permit from the relevant local council. Permits are normally granted for investigation purposes only.

Motoring

A EU Driving Licence is accepted for driving in Spain. If your current one does not comply with the EU format, you are advised to obtain an International Driving Licence, available from the AA. EU citizens are advised to obtain the EU format licence from the Driver's Vehicle Agency. A valid driving licence is required at all times when driving in Spain. The vehicle logbook, registration and adequate insurance are also required. On the spot payment of traffic fines is applicable to non residents.

Museums

All Spanish state museums offer free admission to groups of students or teachers. Permission for free entry must be sought in advance from Ministerio de Cultura, Museums Department, Plaza del Rey, Madrid. Tel: (0034) 917017267 Fax: (0034) 915233687. www.mec.es. Free admission for individual students may also be granted in certain cases to holders of International Student Cards. Further information is available from the Central Bureau for International Education and Training (Tel: 020 7389 4004 Fax: 020 7389 4426. www.centralbureau.org.uk) and the Spanish Cultural Office of the Spanish Embassy.

Pets
An export health certificate issued by an official British Veterinary Inspector is required to import pets into Spain.

Public holidays

1 January	New Year's Day
6 January	King's Day
19 March	St Joseph's Day
Easter	Good Friday and Easter Sunday
1 May	Labour Day
25 July	St James's Day
15 August	Assumption of the Virgin
12 October	National Day
1 November	All Saints Day
6 December	Constitution Day
8 December	Immaculate Conception
25 December	Christmas Day

Shopping
Most shops in Spain close at lunchtime normally between 1.00 p.m. and 4.00 p.m. General stores are to be found in most provincial capital towns. They are open all day from 10.00 a.m. to 8.00 p.m. Open-air markets are held once or twice a week in most Spanish towns and holiday resorts.

Summer time

From the morning of the last Sunday in March to the last Sunday in October.

Taxis

Taxi fares vary in different areas. There is a basic initial charge, a rate per kilometre and additional surcharges added to the meter fare at night, weekends and public holidays. Taxi drivers should have a list of approved fares for inter-city runs, railway stations and airports, and will be able to supply information prior to boarding the vehicle.

Telephone service

To call direct to the UK from Spain, dial 0044 + local UK code without the first 0. Calls to Spain start with 0034. Telephone rates need to be checked locally. Full instructions are shown in all international boxes. Dial 112 for all emergencies.

Television

The Spanish television systems are Norma G for black and white and PAL for colour. British television sets are not suitable for either unless previously adjusted by a technician.

Tipping

5–10% of the bill is customary, although related to clients' satisfaction with the services received.

Vaccinations

No vaccinations are needed by EU residents to enter Spain.

Appendix 3

Contract of Letting

In the City of...............on...............(date)

BETWEEN
On the one part...............with DNI No. ....and
address...

And the other part...............with DNI No. ....and
address...

THEY TAKE PART
The first in name and representing...............(name of
letting company) with CIF.............................and address
....

The second in name and the right as owner of the house/
apartment situated in............... (name of town) with the
property address as..

Both parties are recognised to have the legal capacity to
sign this present contract and,

THEY AGREE
FIRST: That the company stated above is devoted
amongst other activities to the intermediary services of
letting and house maintenance.

SECOND: That the owner wants to sign the present lease with the following,

STIPULATIONS
FIRST: OBJECT: The owner instructs the Company to arrange the contract of letting of the property, collect the rental money and carry out the small repairs and maintenance as are necessary.

SECOND: DURATION: The responsibility for the present Contract of Lease will commence at the signing of this Contract which will be relevant for a period of one year, concluding on...............It is to be understood that the Contract will continue for an equal period of time if neither party cancels the said arrangement by giving at least 15 days' notice.

THIRD: PRICE: The Company will receive as consideration of its services 22.5% of the rental plus IVA, corresponding to that agreed at the time of formalising this Contract.
Payments will be made indicating the rents earned by the apartment less the expenses of the real estate administration and all entered in the accounts presented by the Company.

FOURTH: EXCLUSIVITY: The present contract is carried out exclusively, for the time period of its validity, in favour of............................. Carrying out the letting on behalf of the owner or other concern, the Company receives an indemnity for management, the sum of ....Euros.

FIFTH: INFORMATION: The Company will provide for the Owner, whenever required, any information on the accounts carried out by virtue of this contract.

SIXTH: WRONG USE OF THE APARTMENT: Any breakages or damages for bad or inappropriate use will be the responsibility of the tenant who has hired the property by Contract from...

All parties, in proof of the agreement, sign contract, in duplicate, in the place and date mentioned above.

Signature...............   Signature...............

Appendix 4

Arrienda de Temporada
(Contract for Short Term Letting)

In the City of...............on...............(date)

On the one part, the owner of...........................with DNI No...............or Passport No...............and address...

....

And the other part................with habitual residence in the city of................ and address....................................

Both parties are recognised to have the legal capacity to agree this present **CONTRACT OF LEASE FOR SHORT TERM LETTING** with the following **CLAUSES**:

1. The object of the letting is the apartment in Apartment Block...............Number............... Street...............which is furnished and equipped as indicated on the Inventory together with this Contract of Letting that forms part of the same.

2. The letting of this apartment is agreed for the inclusive period from...............to............... On the final day of the agreed period of letting the contract is automatically dissolved and cannot be extended.

3. The price for the period of letting within the validity of this contract is...............Euros monthly. It is agreed that the services of water and garbage removal are included in the rental price. The cost of electricity is extra.

4. The person renting agrees, on the termination of the contract, to leave the apartment in identical condition as received on entry, with the furniture and equipment as itemised on the inventory and that any necessary repairs or replacement of lost or damaged items will be to the account of the renter.

5. The owner holds to the renter's account the sum of ....Euros as a deposit to use in the event Clause 4 above has not been adhered to. In the event that the apartment is left in the same condition as from the first day of the contract then the deposit will be returned to the renter. This contract is a receipt for said deposit.

6. It is forbidden that the lessee:

a) Sublets or reassigns the apartment, free or for payment, partial or total.

b) Undertakes any activity outside the norms of usual coexistence, decency and public order.

c) Introduces animals or explosive substances, inflammable or dangerous.

d) Changes the apartment in any way to an end different to that of housing for the period of letting.

7. When the period of the contract has lapsed, the renter will vacate the apartment and return possession of it to the owner. After the end of the said termination of contract all rights previously held by the renter will cease.

8. In the event of any dispute arising from this contract, the parties submit themselves expressly to the Courts and Tribunals of...............

All parties, in proof of agreement, sign the present contract, in duplicate, in the place and date mentioned above.

Signature...............   Signature...............

Appendix 5

Following the Tourist Trail

THE ATTRACTIONS OF A TRADITIONAL FAMILY HOLIDAY

The eastern coast of Spain bordering on the Mediterranean, together with the Balearics and Canaries are Europe's holiday playground. As tourism has developed so too have the amenities. Commercialism is on a terrifying scale, but all designed to let people enjoy, relax and fulfill a sun soaked holiday.

Costa Blanca

One of the big attractions in the Costa Blanca is the recently opened Terra Mitica (Land of Myths), a theme park inspired by the ancient myths of Egypt, Rome, Iberia and Greece. It is possible to step inside the Pyramid of Cheops, experience Triton's Fury with a good soaking and a white-knuckle splashdown or enter the Flight of the Phoenix – a heart stopping 54 metre sheer vertical drop. There are activities for all ages, themed restaurants and costumed hosts.

In Benidorm itself there are performing dolphins, parrots and sea lions at Mundomar, which also has mazy woodland paths to explore. Next door is a huge water park called Aqualandia. A taste of Africa can be obtained at the two drive through safari parks – Safari Park Vergel and Safari Aitana.

Close by, the sun's heat is escaped in the cool Canelobre Caves which features weird and wonderful stalactites.

Costa del Sol

The largest and best of Spain's animal parks is the recently opened Selwo Nature Park at Estepona, home to some 2,000 animals, many of which roam free in semi-wild conditions, amidst various ecosystems. Spot the lions and tigers, rhinos and zebras, hippos in the lake and even rare albino kangaroos. Walk over a bridge, gaze down to the animals below or drive in special safari vehicles.

There are more wild animals in semi-natural conditions at Gocodriles Park, Aljaima, up in the hills behind Malaga. Come face to face with 'Big Nose', a full-grown 77-year old monster crocodile or coo over his newly-hatched descendants.

Tivoli World at Arroyo de la Miel is one of Spain's longest-established theme parks, set in landscaped gardens. White-knuckle rides include roller coasters, the terrifying Tivoli Dragon and the biggest flume ride on the Costa del Sol.

At La Cueva de Nerja, a fantastic cave of cathedral-like proportions, the world's longest stalactite is featured. It says so in *The Guinness Book of Records*.

Mini Hollywood, near Almeria, was the film location for over 100 movies, including *The Magnificent Seven*, *A Fistful of Dollars* and *The Good, the Bad and the Ugly*. Shoot outs, hangings and bank hold-ups – all carefully orchestrated – still take place.

Gibraltar

Everyone enjoys being whisked to the top of the Rock by cable car and then exploring the well interpreted Great Siege Tunnels. Of course, there are those famous Barbary apes, who pose like actors for photos. Do not feed them or try to handle them. A short walk away is St Michael's Cave – a huge natural grotto, with beautifully illuminated giant stalactites and stalagmites.

Mallorca

Forget all that sun, sea and sand. Immerse the mind in the surreal, eerily lit stalactite and stalagmite filled world of the Cuevas del Drac (Caves of the Dragon) on Mallorca's east coast. The trip finishes with an unforgettable concert set on the cave's magical underground lake.

In the sunshine, near Palma Nova, dolphins are the star performers at Marine Land, while sea lions and parrots are given supporting roles. There are also penguins, sharks and tropical fish, monkeys, a reptile house and a large aviary. Creatures without cages roam the Auto Safari at Cala Millor, with giraffes, zebras and monkeys.

Aquacity at S'Arenal claims to be the biggest water park in Europe and also boasts go-karts, falconry demonstrations, mini-zoo, mini-farm and the obligatory parrot show. Splash around at the Hidropark, Port d'Alcudia and the Aquapark at Magaluf.

Tenerife

Top of the attractions is the excellent Loro Parque, in the north of the island at Puerto de la Cruz, which began life as the world's largest collection of bros (parrots), then added more with the biggest dolphinarium outside the USA and the world's longest underwater tunnel. Sealions and parrots also perform; there's a gorilla jungle, bat cave, tigers, crocodiles, king penguins, chimps and a 180-degree cinema – all set in glorious subtropical gardens.

Down south, near Los Cristianos, also in a beautiful subtropical setting, the best wildlife attraction is Las Aguilas del Teide, featuring mostly birds of prey.

One of the island's most fascinating sights is its Drago Milenario, a 1,000 year old Dragon Tree. With a girth of around 20 feet and height of 50 feet it's impressive by any standards.

Aguapark Octopus is the island's best water park – famous for its 'trompe l'oeil' giant orange water tap! It too has a dolphinarium.

Gran Canaria
Wildlife, the Wild West and wild driving are three of the big attractions on Gran Canaria.

Palmitos Parque features over a thousand exotic birds – including performing parrots, a butterfly house, hummingbirds and an orchid house. Crocodilos Park offers more than just 300 crocodiles, with Siberian tigers, performing parrots, snakes, reptiles, an aquarium and a monkey house. There are more snakes, reptiles and assorted creepy crawlies at Reptilandia Park, Galdar.

Sioux City was built as a Western set in the 1960s and has been developed as a small theme park. Cows stampede through the town, the bullets fly and the saloon resounds to the sound of yeehahs!

Holiday World, in the centre of Maspalomas, is a permanent funfair with white-knuckle and gentler rides. Parrots and sea lions do their bit here too. Aqua Sur, near Palmitos Parque, is the largest water park in the Canaries, with 29 different rides. Ocean Park at Maspalomas and Aquapark at Puerto Rico are two other splash-a-minute favourites.

Lanzarote

There is much less in Lanzarote than on the two main Canary Islands. However everyone will enjoy the incredible moonscapes of the Montanas de Fuego (Fire Mountains) National Park, and the guide's party trick of turning a bucket of water into a whooshing geyser. There are also camel rides. Until recently camels were beasts of burden on the islands, but today they are harnessed for tourism and safaris.

SPANISH CITIES

Selling visitors the idea of a short break to Spanish cities is very much a preoccupation of the Tourist Board. Barcelona and Madrid are the most popular, Sevilla is next, followed by Valencia and Palma.

Bilbao, familiar with ferry passengers, has now entered the tourist agenda because of the Guggenheim Museum, together with smaller cities such as Cordoba in Andalucia, and Santiago de Compostela in Galicia.

Art and culture are the two most important factors drawing people to Spanish cities. Visitors enjoy the museums, art galleries, opera, ballet and concerts. Shopping is a secondary attraction, with outlets ranging from major stores to flea markets offering quality and choice at a price likely to be far lower than in the UK.

Spanish cities are alive almost around the clock, and because a large number of people still live in the city centre it is possible to experience typical bars, cafes, shops and markets within walking distance of major museums and other attractions.

Spanish food is gaining a higher profile in the UK with the proliferation of tapas bars, and while they might not be authentic they have raised interest in experiencing the real thing. The tapas bars in Spanish cities are a good choice for the busy tourist, offering delicious snacks at any time if you don't want to wait for lunch after 2.00 p.m. or dinner after 9.00 p.m.

A good choice for solo travellers is Barcelona, a very cosmopolitan city where it easy to make friends and the nightlife goes on until dawn.

GREEN SPAIN

Wild, rugged northern Spain holds secrets beyond the cities, offering visitors the chance to experience a rural countryside with a unique pace of life. Espana Verde – Green Spain – brings together four of the country's autonomous regions. Galicia, Asturias, Cantabria and the Basque Country, situated between the Cantabrian Sea and the Cantabrian mountains. These areas offer an individual identity that reflect a very traditional Spain – nature at its most wild, gourmet food, interesting trails and other activities such as horseback riding, trekking and canoeing.

In Galicia, for example, 1,300 kilometers of rocky coastline is broken by 13 estuaries and dotted by over 700 beaches, while the principality of Asturias – established in the 14th century – has one national park, three natural parks, ten natural reserves, and ten protected landscapes.

RUTAS

Ruta via de la Plata and *Ruta via de la Oro* are two old Roman pathways in the north west of the country. They were built to establish an adequate communications system with the central plateau, crossing the Cantabrian Mountains that separate northern Spain from the rest of the country. The creation of these roads put an end to the isolation northern Spain was suffering and facilitated commercial exchange with its neighbouring regions.

Today the remains of these ancient Roman tracks can be visited. Follow the authentic road as it winds its way from north to south linking the cities of Gijon, Astorga, Salamanca, Caceres, Merida and Sevilla. Along the route there are Roman bridges, arches and theatres to be visited, city walls passed and medieval cities entered. As mountains, valleys and ravines are traversed the heritage of one of the most important parts of the Roman Empire is revealed.

CIUDADES PATRIMONIO DE LA HUMANIDAD DE ESPANA

Spain's World Heritage sites, recognised by UNESCO due to their artistic and cultural wealth are yet another example of tourism being diverted away from the coastal areas. The cities are:

Avila: A 1,000 year old walled city standing at over 1,100 metres high on the southern boundary of the Castilian plateau.

Caceres: In the middle of Extremadura, near Portugal, this city was home to the Romans, Arabs and Christians. It has thousands of coats of arms, all evoking heroic deeds and legends, carved on house walls.

Cordoba: Situated on the banks of the River Guadalquivir this city reached great importance with the arrival of the Moors and became the capital city of Al Andalus. It was a seat of learning. Today thousands of tourists visit, usually stopping at the vast mosque.

Cuenca: Its hanging houses are famous world wide but its setting on imposing limestone rock is equally unusual.

Salamanca: Not too far from Portugal this dynamic, cosmopolitan city is home to young students filling its prestigious university.

Santiago de Compostela: Its proximity to the sea in north east Spain gives a mild and wet climate to those who wish to undertake a pilgrimage to this historic city with its notable cathedral.

Segovia: The Romans recognised the strategic nature of this location, building an aqueduct some 2,000 years ago. This true wonder of engineering is over 700 metres long, has 166 arches but is still off the tourist trail.

Toledo: A city located in the centre of Spain, its origins going back to a long and remote past. It has a maze of narrow streets, synagogues, mosques, museums and the River Tagus. It is famous for steel swords.

Sources: Spanish Tourist Board, *Mediterranean Life* and others.

Appendix 6

Case Study – Business Plan

Background
Detailed in Chapter 1 Case study – Castles in the Air.

Location
Castell de Castells, Alicante, Spain. Detailed in Chapter 5 Case study – A Special Place.

Property
Newly built on an old site the property sits high above the road that passes on the outskirts of the village. The views are fabulous giving a sense of peace and tranquillity.

The top floor is a garage and summer lounge with settees, desk, TV/DVD and access to the large sun terrace from which to gaze at the lovely scenery in the evening.

Down a flight of stairs is the master bedroom (a bit different this – king size bed on a raised platform) and en-suite bathroom. The adjacent area has masses of ward-robe space linking to the second double bedroom which has a small balcony overlooking the valley and mountains. There is a second separate bathroom.

Down another flight of stairs and you are in the 'family room'. It has a huge table with cupboards below, a fridge, a double sink, an electric hob and oven, a microwave and a small oven for small things! To keep warm there is a traditional Spanish wood burning stove for cold days (the wood is stored under the house) and two settees, one of which turns easily into a very comfortable double bed.

Tenant market
Castell de Castells is situated in one of the best areas for hiking in Spain. Rugged limestone mountains reaching to 5,000 feet surround the village. Access is by ancient mule tracks, Mozarabic trails and dry riverbeds. There are several routes available from the village and many, many more just a short car journey away. The hiking is mostly moderate to easy.

Promotion
- Advertising in UK hiking magazines.
- Tourist Board promotion under *Casa Rurales*.
- Individual and holiday company websites.
- Small, local UK advertisements.
- Word of mouth Spain, UK, and USA.

Competition
In the village there is a hotel, which takes walking groups, a *casa rural*, a pension specialising in mountain bike riding and a few other properties for let. The local Mayoress owns the hotel. Everyone helps each other.

Financial objectives
Maintain a positive cash flow over the initial 5 years against a background of the following facts and assumptions.

The property cost 118,000 Euros which includes the basic shell price, legal fees, building costs, fitting out and bank charges. It does not include the owner's labour costs. It was financed by a 95% mortgage of 112,000 Euros. Property value inflation is assumed to be a very prudent 10% per annum and is included in the theoretical profit calculation but not in the cash flow projections. Letting is for 30 weeks per year at 300 Euros per week with all bookings from advertising and Internet.

Year	1	2	3	4	5
Letting revenue	4500	9000	9000	9000	9000
less					
Advertising	500	500	500	500	500
Mortgage	4000	4000	4000	4000	4000
Agency letting fees	0	0	0	0	0
Insurance	150	150	150	150	150
Depreciation	800	800	800	800	800
Maintenance/decoration	200	300	400	500	600
Utilities	300	400	400	400	400
Admin expenses	200	200	200	200	200
Cleaning	350	700	700	700	700
Taxes	1250	2500	2500	2500	2500
Other	0	0	0	0	0
Total	7750	9550	9650	9750	9850
Trading profit	−3250	−550	−650	−750	−850
Property inflation	12980	14278	15705	17277	19004
Theoretical profit	9730	13728	15045	16527	18154

Figure 16. Profit and loss projection (all figures in Euros).

Year	1	2	3	4	5
Trading profit	−3250	−550	−650	−750	−850
Depreciation	800	800	800	800	800
Opening bank balance	−6000	−8450	−7650	−7500	−7450
Closing balance	−8450	−7650	−7500	−7450	−7400

Figure 17. Cash flow projection (all figures in Euros).

Business ratios

Rent/price ratio	$= 1,300/118,000 \times 100$	$= 1.1\%$
Yield (year 2)	$= -550/143,000 \times 100$	$= 0$
Return (year 2)	$= -550/6,000 \times 100$	$= 0$
Expense ratio	$= 9500/15,600 \times 100$	$= 61\%$
GIM	$= 118/9000 \times 100$	$= 13$ years

Appendix 7

The Communities of Spain and Their Provinces

The provinces of Spain are grouped into 17 autonomous Communities. Asturias is a *Principado*, Murcia is a *Region*, Navarra is a *Comunidad Foral* while all the rest are classified as *Comunidades*. The name, address, the first two digits of the provincial postcode and the provincial letters used on vehicle number plates are shown below.

Northern Spain

Comunidad Galicia, Palacio de Rojoy, 15705 Santiago de Compostela

Galicia	15	A Coruna	C
	27	Lugo	LU
	32	Ourense	OR
	36	Pontevedra	PO

Principado de Asturias, Calle Suarez de la Riva, 33071 Oviedo

Asturias	33	Austurias	O

Comunidad Cantabria, Calle Casimiro Sainz 4, 39003 Santander

Cantabria	39	Cantabria	S

Comunidad Pais Vasco, Palacio de Ajuna-Enea, 01007
Vitoria

Basque	01	Alava	VI
	20	Guipuzcoa	SS
	48	Vizcaya	BI

Comunidad Foral de Navarra, 31002 Pamplona

| Navarra | 31 | Navarra | NA |

Comunidad La Rioja, Calle General Vara del Rey 3,
26071, Logrono

| La Rioja | 26 | La Rioja | LO |

Eastern Spain
Comunidad Cataluna, Plaza de San Jaime, 08002
Barcelona

Catalonia	08	Barcelona	BA
	25	Lleida	L
	17	Girona	GE
	43	Tarragona	T

Comunidad Aragon, Diputacion de Aragon, Paseo Maria
Agustin 36, 50071 Zaragoza

Aragon	22	Huesca	HU
	44	Teruel	TE
	50	Zaragoza	Z

Comunidad Valencia, Palau de la Generalitat, 46003
Valencia

Valencia	03	Alicante	A
	46	Valencia	V
	12	Castellon	CS

Region de Murcia, Palacio de San Esteban, Calle Acisco Diaz, 30071 Murcia

Murcia	30	Murcia	MU

Central Spain

Comunidad Madrid, Puerta del Sol 7, 28013 Madrid

Madrid	28	Madrid	M

Comunidad Castilla La Mancha, Palacio de Fuensalida, Plaza de Conde 2, 45002 Toledo

Castilla la Mancha	02	Albacete	AB
	13	Ciudad Real	CR
	16	Cuenca	CE
	19	Guadalajara	GU
	45	Toledo	TO

Comunidad Extremadura, Calle Jose Fernandez Lopez 18, 06800 Merida

Extremadura	06	Badajoz	BA
	10	Caceres	CC

Comunidad Castilla y Leon, Plaza de Castilla y Leon, 47006 Valladolid

Castilla y Leon	05	Avila	AV
	09	Burgos	BU
	24	Leon	LE
	34	Palencia	P
	37	Salamanca	SA
	40	Segovia	SG
	42	Soria	SO
	47	Valladolid	VA
	49	Zamora	ZA

Southern Spain

Comuidad Andalucia, Palacio de San Telmo, Avda de Roma, 41071, Sevilla

Andalucia	04	Almeria	AL
	11	Cadiz	CA
	14	Cordoba	CO
	18	Granada	GR
	21	Huelva	H
	23	Jaen	J
	29	Malaga	MA
	41	Sevilla	SE

Islands

Comunidad las Islas Balaeres, Calle Marina 3, Consulado del Mar, 07012 Palma de Mallorca

Balearic Islands	07	Baleares	PM

Comunidad las Islas Canarias, Plaza 25 de Julio 1, 35004 Las Palmas de Gran Canaria

Canary Islands	35	Las Palmas	GC
	37	Tenerife	TF

Appendix 8

English Language Newspapers and Magazines

Absolute Marbella
Edificio Tembo, Calle Rotary Internacional, 29660 Puerto Banus, Marbella
Tel: 952908617
www.absolute-marbella.com

Costa Blanca News
Apartado 95, 03500 Benidorm
Tel: 966812841 www.costablanca-news.com

Costa del Sol News
Apartado 102, 29630 Benalmadena Costa (Malaga)
Tel: 952449250 costasol@dragonet.es

Costa Golf
Martinez Campos 16, 29001 Malaga
Tel: 952224931 webmaster@servicios-gi.es

Lookout
Urb. Molino de Viento, Calle Rio Darro, Portal 1, 29650 Mijas
Tel: 952473090 lookout@jet.es

Spain
21 Royal Circus, Edinburgh EH3 6TL
Tel: 0131 2267766 www.spainmagazine.info

Sur in English
    Avda Doctor Maranon 48, 29009 Malaga
    Tel: 952649600 www.surinenglish.com

The Broadsheet
    Bear Publishing, Plaza de Canalejas 6, 28014 Madrid
    Tel: 915237480

The Mallorca Daily Bulletin
    San Filiu 25, Palma de Mallorca

The Island Gazette
Calle Iriarte 43, Santa Cruz, Tenerife

A full list of all English-language publications in Spain
can be found on the website www.spainview.com

Appendix 9

Major Contacts in the UK and Ireland

London Residential Research
151 Waldour Street
London W1F 8WN

Spanish Embassy in the UK
39 Chesham Place
London SW1X 8SB
Tel: 020 7235 5555
Fax: 020 7259 5392

Spanish Consulate General in London
20 Draycott Place
London SW3 2RZ
Tel: 020 7589 8989
Fax: 020 7581 7888

Spanish Consulate General in Manchester
Suite 1A Brookhouse
70 Spring Gardens
Manchester M2 2BQ
Tel: 0161 2361262
Fax: 0161 2287467

Spanish Consulate General in Edinburgh
63 North Castle Street
Edinburgh EH2 3LI
Tel: 0131 2201843
Fax: 0131 2264568

Spanish Consulate General in Dublin
17a Merlyn Park
Ballsbridge
Dublin 4
Tel: 0035 1269 1640
Fax: 0035 1269 1854

Spanish Commercial Office
66 Chiltern Street
London W1U 4LS
Tel: 020 7486 0101
Fax: 020 7487 5586
www.mcx.es/londres
They deal with the promotion of all Spanish products and
have specific departments for food, wine and trade fairs.

Spanish Chamber of Commerce
1 Harley Street
London W1M 0DP
Tel: 020 7637 9061
Fax: 020 7436 7188
www.spanishchamber.co.uk
Will assist with advice on business deals in Spain or with
Spanish exporters in the UK.

Labour Office of the Spanish Embassy
20 Peel Street
London W8 7PD
Tel: 020 7221 0098
Fax: 020 7229 7270
For advice on regulations regarding work and Social
Security in Spain.

Education Office
20 Peel Street
London W8 7PD
Tel: 020 7727 2462
Fax: 020 7229 4965
www.cec-spain.org.uk

Appendix 10

Major Contacts in Spain

Abbey National Offshore
PO Box 824
237 Main St, Gibraltar
Tel: 0035 076090
gibmortgage@abbeyoffshore.com

The Royal Bank of Scotland (Gibraltar) Ltd
PO Box 766
Corral Road
Gibraltar
Tel: 0035 044166
www.focusgibraltar.com

British Chamber of Commerce Spain
Calle Bruc 21
08010 Barcelona
Tel: 933173220
Fax: 933024896
www.britchamberspain.com

British Embassy in Madrid
Calle Fernando el Santo 16
28010 Madrid
Tel: 917008200
Fax: 917008272

British Consulate in Alicante
Plaza de Calvo Sotelo 1-2°
Apdo. de Correos 564
03001 Alicante
Tel: 965216190
Fax: 965140528

British Consulate General in Barcelona
Avenida Diagonal 477-13°
08036 Barcelona
Tel: 933666200
Fax: 933666221

Honorary Vice Consul in Benidorm
Contact – British Consulate in Alicante

British Consulate General in Bilbao
Alameda de Urquijo 2-8°
48008 Bilbao
Tel: 944157600
Fax: 944167632

British Consulate in Cadiz (Honorary)
Union Maritima Espanola S.A.,
Avda Ramon de Carranza 27
11006 Cadiz
Tel: 956264479
Fax: 956286909

British Vice Consulate in Ibiza
Avda de Isidoro Macabich 45-1°
07800 Ibiza

Tel: 971301818
Fax: 971301972

British Consulate in Las Palmas de Gran Canaria
Edificio Cataluna
Calle Luis Morote 6-3°
35007 Las Palmas
Tel: 928262508
Fax: 928267774

British Consulate General in Madrid
Calle Marques de la Ensenada 16,
28004 Madrid
Tel: 913085201
Fax: 913080882

British Consulate in Malaga
Edificio Eurocom, Bloque Sur,
Calle Mauricio Moro Pareto 2-2°
29006 Malaga
Tel: 952352300
Fax: 952359211

British Vice Consulate in Menorca
Sa Casa Nova
Cami de Biniatap 30
07720 Es Castell
Menorca
Tel: 971363373
Fax: 971354690

British Consulate in Palma de Mallorca
Plaza Mayor 3
07002 Palma de Mallorca
Tel: 971712445
Fax: 971717520

British Consulate in Santa Cruz de Tenerife
Plaza Weyler 8
38003 Santa Cruz de Tenerife
Tel: 922286863
Fax: 922289903

British Consulate in Santander (Honorary)
Paseo de Pereda 27
39004 Santander
Tel: 942220000
Fax: 942222941
Initial enquiries to be directed to British Consulate
General in Bilbao

British Consulate in Sevilla (Honorary)
Apartado de Correos
POBox 143
41940 Tomares (Sevilla)
Initial enquiries to be directed to British Consulate in
Malaga

British Consulate in Vigo (Honorary)
Plaza Compostela 23-6°
36201 Vigo
Tel: 986437133
Fax: 986437133

Honorary Consular Agent Granada
Plaza San Cristobal
18010 Granada
Tel: 669895053
Fax: 958274724

Embassy of Ireland
Ireland House
Paseo de la Castellana
46-4°, 28046 Madrid
Tel: 915763500
Fax: 914351677

Ireland Honorary Vice Consul, Barcelona
Gran Via Carlos 94
08028 Barcelona
Tel: 934519021
Fax: 934112921

Ireland Honorary Consul, Malaga
Galerias Santa Monica,
Avenida Los Boliches 15
29640 Fuengirola
Malaga
Tel: 952466783
Fax: 952466783

Appendix 11

Useful Websites

Accommodation – paradores, hotels and spas

Asociacion de Termales	www.balnearios.org
Hotusa Hotels	www.hotusa.es
Husa Hotels	www.husa.es
Novotel	www.novotel.com
Paradores	www.paradores.es
Santos Hotels	www.h-santos.es
Sol Melia Hotels	www.solmelia.es
Tryp Hotels	www.tryp.es

Financial planning

Blevins and Franks	www.blevinsfranks.com
Henry Woods	www.henrywoods.com
Sovereign Group Spain	www.sovereigngroup.com

News and information

BBC World Service	www.bbc.uk/worldservice
British Council	www.britishcouncil.es
British Executive Service Overseas	www.beso.org
Central Intelligence Agency	www.cia.gov/cia/publications/ factbook
Language translation	www.fodors.com/language
Stanford's (maps, guides and travel books)	

www.stanfords.co.uk

Pets

Department of
Environment   www.defra.gov.uk/animalh/
                     quarantine

Property rental

(a selection of some of the best websites)

www.brittany-ferries.com
www.europropertysearch.com
www.euro-rentavilla.com
www.holidayhome.co.uk
www.holidayrentals.co.uk
www.privatevillas.co.uk
www.ownersdirect.co.uk
www.ownerssyndicate.co.uk
www.holidaybank.com
www.simplyspanish.com

Property sales

Atlas International	www.atlas-international.com
David Headland	
Associates	www.headland.co.uk
Masa International	
UK Ltd	www.masainter.com
Propertunities Ltd	www.propertunities.co.uk
Spanish private sales	www.loot.com
Taylor Woodrow	www.taywoodspain.co.uk
Ultra Villas	www.ultravillas.co.uk

Retirement

Occupational Pensions Registry	www.opra.co.uk
UK State pensions	www.dss.gov.uk

Sports

General	www.csd.mec.es
	www.spanish-living.com
	www.aboutspain.net
Golf	www.golfspainfederation.com
	www.golfspain.com
Tennis	www.fedetenis.es
	www.playtennispain.com
Water sports	www.rfev.es
	www.windsurfspain.com

Taxation

Inland Revenue, (former UK tax payers now living abroad)
Fitzroy House, PO Box 46
Nottingham NG2 1BD   www.inlandrevenue.gov.uk

Tourist offices

Andalucia	www.andalucia.org
Aragon	www.staragon.com
Asturias	www.infoasturias.com
Baleric Islands	www.caib.es
Canary Islands	www.godcan.es
Cantabria	www.turismo.cantabria.org
Castilla la Mancha	www.jccm.es
Castilla y Leon	www.jcyl.es
Cataluna	www.gencat.es/probert
Extremadura	www.tourismoextremadura.com

Galicia	www.tourgalicia.es
La Rioja	www.larioja.org
Madrid	www.comadrid.es
Murcia	www.carm.es
Navarra	www.cfnavarra.es
Pais Vasco	www.euskadi.net
Valenciana	www.comunidad-valenciana.org
General	www.tourspain.es
	www.tourspain.co.uk
	Info.londres@toursppain.es
Gibraltar Tourist Board	www.gibraltar.gi

Travel and flights

Air Lingus	www.aerlingus.com
British Airways	www.britishairways.com
British Airways Authority	www.baa.co.uk
Brittany Ferries (Plymouth to Santander)	www.brittanyferries.com
Easy Jet	www.easyJet.com
Eurostar	www.eurostar.com
Eurotunnel	www.eurotunnel.com
Foreign Office Travel Advice	www.fco.gov.uk/travel
GB Airways	www.gbairways.com
Iberia	www.iberia.com
P&O (Portsmouth to Bilbao)	www.poportsmouth.com
Spanish Railways	www.renfe.com

Appendix 12

Further Reading

SPANISH HISTORY

Don Quixote, Miguel Cervantes (Penguin). A classic
Modern Spain, Raymond Carr (Opus). Says it all
The New Spaniards, John Hooper (Penguin). An excellent work
The Spanish Tragedy, Raymond Carr (Phoenix). The civil war in perspective

SPANISH CULTURE

Culture Shock, Marie Louise Graff (Kuperard). A guide to Spanish customs and etiquettes
Death in the Afternoon, Earnest Hemingway (Grafton). His famous look at bullfighting
Spain, Jan Morris (Faber and Faber), Writing at its best
The Sun also Rises, Earnest Hemmingway (Grafton). Fiestas

BUYING A PROPERTY IN SPAIN

Buying a House in Spain, David Hampshire (Survival). A jocular style
Buying a Property in Spain, Harry King (How To Books). An easy to read guide
Living in Spain, (Bill Blevins and David Franks). Financial affairs
You and the Law in Spain, David Searle (Santana). Detailed

RENTING PROPERTY

Buy, Rent and Sell, Robert Irwin (McGraw Hill). How they do it in the USA

How to Buy and Manage Rental Property, Mike Milin (Fireside). 200 properties in the USA

Making Money from Holiday Lets: Jackie Taylor (How To Books). A start up handbook

Making Money from Letting: Moira Stewart (How To Books). Letting property in the UK

GOING TO SPAIN

Best Places to Buy a Home in Spain, Joanna Styles (Survival). All the facts

Going to Live in Spain, Harry King, (How To Books). Another straightforward guide

Living and Working in Spain, David Hampshire (Survival). A fact filled guide

Retire Abroad, Roger Jones (How To books). Happy retirement abroad

LEARNING THE LANGUAGE

AA Essential Spanish Phrase Book (AA). Common sense phrases

Oxford Spanish Starter Dictionary (Oxford University Press)

Suenos World Spanish (BBC). Multi media course for beginners

Viva Espana (BBC). Beginners language course

TRAVEL

Eyewitness Spain (Dorling and Kindersley). The best travel guide

Spain, Dana Facaros and Michael Pauls (Cadogan

Guides). A different style

Special Places to Stay, Alastair Sawday (ASP). A roof off the beaten track

Sunflower Landscapes (Sunflower Books). Four walking guides for Spain

FOOD AND WINE

Cooking in Spain, Janet Mendal (Santana). The essential cooking book for Spain

Tapas and More Great Dishes from Spain, Janet Mendal (Santana). Spain's bar food

The New Spain, John Radford (Mitchell Beazley). A well-illustrated wine guide

World Food Spain (Lonely Planet). Buying fun food

HUMOUR

Driving Over Lemons, Chris Stewart (Sort of Book). A humorous optimist in Andalucia

A Parrot in a Pepper Tree, Chris Stewart (Sort of Book). His lesser sequel

Nord Riley's Spain, Nord Riley (Santana). The life of a humorous wanderer

Spanish Lessons, Derek Lambert (Embury). Beginning a new life in Spain

KEEPING HEALTHY

Health and Illness in Retirement, Anne Roberts (Ace Books). Recommended

Tell the Doctor, Calle El Moreral 3, 03792 Parcent, Alicante. A home publication only available by post

We are in Hospital (Alicante University/Cam Bank). One for the bookshelf

RESEARCH

Sunset Lives, King, Warnes, Williams (Berg). Retirement Migration to the Mediterranean

Dr Tony Warnes (Sheffield University). Various research papers

British on the Costa del Sol, Karen O'Reilly (Routledge). Little England in Spain.

Index